Adolf Loos: Meaning, Context, Reception
Essays

Christopher Long

Adolf Loos: Meaning, Context, Reception

Essays

Christopher Long

KANT

For Francesco Passanti

Contents

Portrait of Adolf Loos by Benedikt Fred Doblin. From B. F. Doblin, *Österreichische Profile* (Munich: Albert Langen–George Müller Verlag, 1959), 18.

Preface

I wrote all but two of the essays in this book in 2021 and 2022, during the time of the worldwide Covid-19 pandemic. A shortened version of one of the essays, "Adolf Loos and the Lessons of the Vernacular," appeared in the *Festschrift* for Jindřich Vybíral, *Umění a evoloce: Sborník pro Jindřicha Vybírala*, published in 2020.[1] And I completed most of the "The Iconic Tower" in 2016, though I did not publish it at that time. I had no particular purpose in writing these pieces, other than to work out ideas—or clusters of thoughts—I have had in my head for many years. I have now written all or part of five books on Loos, but I can't quite rid myself of him, his work, or his ideas.

Two ideas have been much in the forefront of my mind in the past several years. The first involves perhaps Loos's most brilliant insight: that architecture and design (and by extension everything we use and everything that frames our daily lives) are inextricably bound up with our culture—that these things are not merely the reflection of a given culture but arise directly from it. That simple but profound thought guided Loos throughout his working life.

The second of Loos's legacies has to do with his notions of pluralism and continuity. Loos is probably correct when he claims that art and design go off track when they cease being a product of a collective will and become too "individualized." Yet even more arresting is his suggestion that one of the key aspects of modern life is that it contains everything that led up to it. It makes no sense to contrive a perfect style or a unified way of living. What arises from this insight, if we push it to its logical end, is quite useful: that one of the preconditions of modernity is pluralism. Loos did not understand this as we might today—in the cloak of a full-blown multiculturalism. Loos was still very much a turn-of-the-century European in his outlook, and a strong whiff of Eurocentrism pervades his writings. Still, Loos perceived with remarkable precision that our time is wrapped up with a persistent multifariousness, that there is more than one way to be and live in an authentically modern way. It is an important reminder, even if we must now regard it from a very different, global perspective.

These ideas are present many of these essays. But there is also more, about Loos the man, and, especially, about Loos the architect.

Taos, August 2022

1 | A Cultural Approach Notwithstanding

Trotzdem, the second of Adolf Loos's books of essays, was first published in 1930.[1] Its title comes from a quote from the philosopher Friedrich Nietzsche, "daß Alles Entscheidende 'trotzdem' entsteht" (All which is decisive happens "nonetheless")[2]

For Loos, the word *trotzdem*—"notwithstanding" or "in spite of," as it might also be translated—was a pronouncement of defiance. It was, even more, a declaration of his supposed victory over his opponents. By the time the book appeared, he had weathered some three decades of criticism and abuse (which Loos was quite adept at hurling himself), and his vision of modernism had at last triumphed.

Or so he thought. Loos had won a great victory over those who, around the turn of the century, had insisted that the true path to modernism lay in the invention of a novel style—the Art Nouveau or Jugendstil. That version of modernism had long since come and gone; by 1930, it looked quaint at best. Yet Loos's belief in a modernism that had arisen on its own, that was not contrived but was an authentic expression of modern life, that still left a place for those objects from the past that retained some validity and usefulness—that vision of modernism was far from the dominant ideal in 1930. And so it would be ever after.

Trotzdem was something more for Loos. It was a statement of his belief about how cultures evolve. It was his key to understanding how life and its trappings changed over time. It was not an explanation of how style evolved. Loos was much less concerned with that issue; for him, style was epiphenomenal. Rather, it was an assertion of inevitability. Loos believed that one feature above all defines cultural evolution: it is relentless; it is unstoppable. New cultures arose when the circumstances of daily living changed, and such change, in turn, triggered a shift in beliefs, aspirations, and practices. Modernism had come into being, so Loos thought, because the conditions of life—especially urban life—had been transformed, and with this transformation had come an alteration in people's perceptions about how they should live, dress, eat, and build.

On the face of it, these are simple ideas. Cultural change is inexorable; cultural change is an expression of the realities and needs of daily life. Yet embedded in these ideas are two other vital insights. These insights would not only define Loos's thinking concerning modernity and its meanings; they would also provide the guide for nearly every one of his design decisions.

The first is that the engine of cultural change is not individual will or action. Cultural change is instead the result of collective experience. It is born of many thousands of daily interactions and decisions. As human beings, we institute a culture together, for culture is always shared. Because our experiences are similar, as the conditions of life change so do our ideas of how to live and how to constitute our surroundings.

Loos's second great insight might sound prosaic, even banal: cultural evolution is just that. It involves change over time, sometimes gradual, sometimes sudden. But never does it signal a complete shift. Some forms and ideas from the past will persist, even while others are supplanted. Just as in biological evolution (a subject that interested Loos) some vestigial features always remained as a life form evolved, so too would that be the case with cultural evolution.

What this means, if one takes the idea seriously, is that modernism could never have amounted to a wholesale transformation. There would always be past forms, as well as past habits and beliefs, present in any given age or place. Even more, it meant that modern life could not be *invented*. It was the outcome of a broad and unavoidable process involving the many, not the few.

Loos came to these ideas slowly. It took him more than a decade to develop his concept of cultural evolution, and he never expressed it completely in any individual writing. To see it in its totality means combining multiple strands woven into his essays. But the seeds of Loos's great insights were there from the outset. Even in his first essays, one can discern the flickers of his later thinking on culture and its meanings.

Loos was twenty-five years old when he moved to Vienna in the late summer of 1896. He had spent the previous three years in the United States. That experience—and what came immediately after—would be central to his developing ideas.

His advanced formal education in architecture had been adequate at best—two years at the Staatsgewerbeschule (State Trades School) in Brünn (Brno), where he studied "building" (the school in Brno was set up primarily to train master builders), and then two years in the architecture department at the Technische Hochschule, or polytechnic university, in Dresden. He had probably gleaned a good deal about construction and design by the time he left Dresden: the school had a reputation for teaching the newest methods of building and stylistic appropriation. But Loos was far from a fully-fledged architect when he departed for the United States in early July 1893. And his education in other areas—in the humanities, for example—was weak, arrested by the fact that for most of his early teenage years he had been shunted from one Gymasium to the next (largely because he kept getting expelled) and because of his deafness, which by this time was already advanced.

What Loos seems to have possessed, though, was a powerful capacity to observe the world around him, down to the smallest details. This is not unusual: people often find that as one of their senses fades or departs altogether, others become stronger, more acute. Loos seemingly watched and thought about everything in his world intensely because he frequently couldn't hear what was going on. Loos's great skill, however, was discerning patterns and their meanings. He had an innate gift for thinking about the broader implications of the profound alterations—cultural, social, economic, and artistic—he saw taking place around him.

He did this, as I have said, by observing intently. He was never an especially avid or systematic reader. He read what interested him, mostly about topics that were *Tagesgespräch*—"the talk of the day," or as we would say, current events. He seems to have picked up this book or that article and read it only insofar as it occupied his interest. He apparently came to many of his topics through the writers Peter Altenberg and Karl Kraus, the two close friends of his early Vienna years. Kraus, in particular, though younger than Loos by some four years, seems often to have played the part of his intellectual Virgil.

One of the books Loos apparently did read was Max Nordau's *Entartung* (Degeneration), published in two volumes in 1892 and 1893.[3] Loos likely encountered the book shortly after his return from America, in 1896 or 1897, when it was still being read and actively discussed in Vienna. It formed the intellectual bedrock of his cultural worldview.

Nordau's assault on the injurious impacts of modern life was focused on Paris. The shockwaves of rapid urbanization and the stresses of modern life on humans, their art, and their culture, were equally valid for Vienna, which had undergone precipitous growth—and all the attendant tensions that produced—over the previous three or four decades. Nordau, who was a trained physician, believed these stresses were leading to a form of mental illness: degeneration. And Nordau declared that degeneration was a direct product of the phenomenon of fin-de-siècle Europe. Its specific manifestations were a tendency toward mysticism, world-weariness, and "decadent" forms of art. Those who were afflicted were deviant and required therapy. A significant portion of his book is devoted to case studies of those Nordau believed were so affected: Hendrik Ibsen, Friedrich Nietzsche, Oscar Wilde, and Richard Wagner.

Loos seems to have taken two direct lessons from Nordau's diagnosis of the ills of turn-of-the-century culture. The first was that the changes of the late nineteenth century, upending old values and practices, would inevitably lead to some sort of response; second, and more significantly, one of the chief responses was a tendency on the part of artists and intellectuals to find refuge in artifice, rather than a headlong response to reality.

Loos must have also seen something else in Nordau: an inclination to think broadly about culture and cultural change. Nordau's book was not the only source for such thinking; in the late 1890s, European writing was replete with references to culture and its meanings. And *Kultur* was especially prominent in the German-language publications of the day. But Nordau's specific equation of culture and crisis seems to have been formative for Loos.

It was in this period, too, that Loos must have become familiar with Darwinism and the social Darwinism of Herbert Spencer. And we know from his later writings that Loos had at least a passing understanding of Cesare Lombroso's ideas about the relationship between criminality and a criminal's mental defects. He also took in the writings about the recent discoveries of "primitive" peoples in Papua New Guinea.[4]

It is what Loos did with this motley concoction of ideas—some crackpot, others rather more on the mark—that made him the compelling theorist he

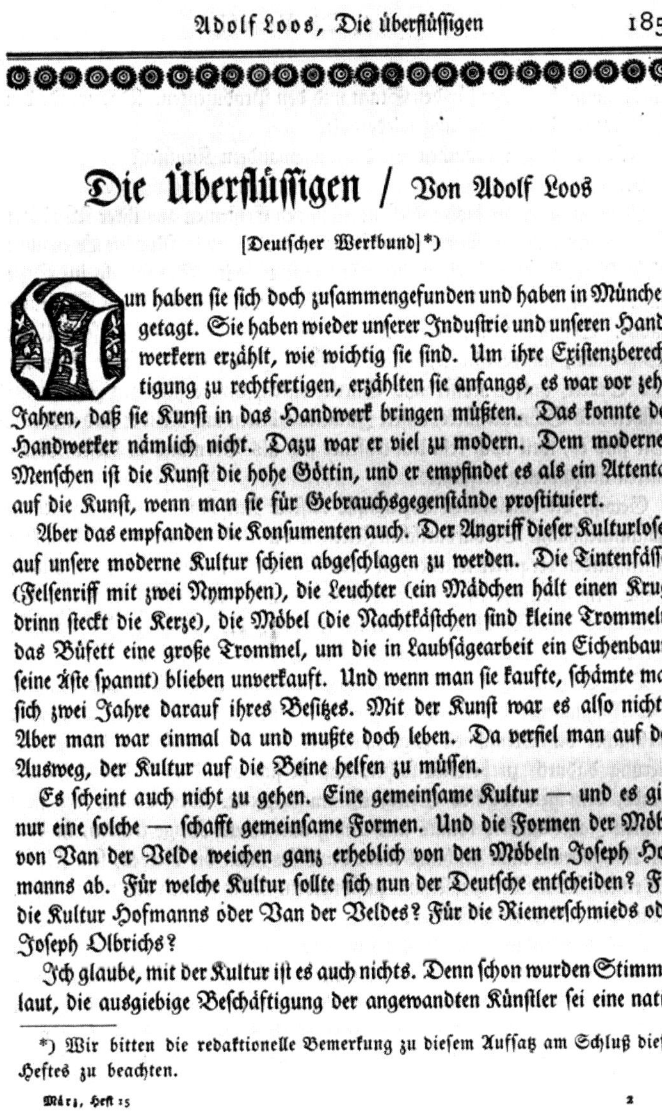

Die Überflüssigen / Von Adolf Loos

[Deutscher Werkbund]*)

Nun haben sie sich doch zusammengefunden und haben in München getagt. Sie haben wieder unserer Industrie und unseren Handwerkern erzählt, wie wichtig sie sind. Um ihre Existenzberechtigung zu rechtfertigen, erzählten sie anfangs, es war vor zehn Jahren, daß sie Kunst in das Handwerk bringen müßten. Das konnte der Handwerker nämlich nicht. Dazu war er viel zu modern. Dem modernen Menschen ist die Kunst die hohe Göttin, und er empfindet es als ein Attentat auf die Kunst, wenn man sie für Gebrauchsgegenstände prostituiert.

Aber das empfanden die Konsumenten auch. Der Angriff dieser Kulturlosen auf unsere moderne Kultur schien abgeschlagen zu werden. Die Tintenfässer (Felsenriff mit zwei Nymphen), die Leuchter (ein Mädchen hält einen Krug, drinn steckt die Kerze), die Möbel (die Nachtkästchen sind kleine Trommeln, das Büfett eine große Trommel, um die in Laubsägearbeit ein Eichenbaum seine Äste spannt) blieben unverkauft. Und wenn man sie kaufte, schämte man sich zwei Jahre darauf ihres Besitzes. Mit der Kunst war es also nichts. Aber man war einmal da und mußte doch leben. Da verfiel man auf den Ausweg, der Kultur auf die Beine helfen zu müssen.

Es scheint auch nicht zu gehen. Eine gemeinsame Kultur — und es gibt nur eine solche — schafft gemeinsame Formen. Und die Formen der Möbel von Van der Velde weichen ganz erheblich von den Möbeln Joseph Hofmanns ab. Für welche Kultur sollte sich nun der Deutsche entscheiden? Für die Kultur Hofmanns oder Van der Veldes? Für die Riemerschmieds oder Joseph Olbrichs?

Ich glaube, mit der Kultur ist es auch nichts. Denn schon wurden Stimmen laut, die ausgiebige Beschäftigung der angewandten Künstler sei eine natio-

*) Wir bitten die redaktionelle Bemerkung zu diesem Aufsatz am Schluß dieses Heftes zu beachten.

| 1.1. First page of Loos's essay "Die Überflüssigen" (The Superfluous Ones). From *März* 2, no. 15 (August 1908): 185.

became. He began to think *culturally*. He saw the profound disruptions of the industrial age not through an economic lens, as Karl Marx had done, or with a purely social looking glass à la Spencer. He rejected, too, the strident individualism of Nietzsche, Nordau, and Sigmund Freud. Loos—rather remarkably given his peripatetic education—instead began to discern a set of patterns about culture and cultural change that led him to develop his own distinctive views.

This cluster of ideas, especially his belief that an alteration in collective experience and outlook precedes cultural change, is present in nearly all his writings and designs, sometimes explicitly, sometimes simply in the background. But to get at the heart of Loos's cultural argument we can concentrate on just three of his essays.

The first is "Die Überflüssigen," or "The Superfluous Ones" (fig. 1.1). Loos wrote the essay in response to what he had witnessed while attending the first meeting of the Deutscher Werkbund, which was held in Munich on October 5 and 6, 1907. It was published the following year in the Munich-based cultural and literary journal *März*, whose editors included Hermann Hesse.[5]

The piece is broadly satirical—as so many of Loos's essays were—but it makes several salient points that relate to his cultural outlook. The Werkbund was an effort on the part of the German reformers to bring together some of the country's leading manufacturers and designers in a formal working alliance. Its stated goal was to better the quality of German goods and make them more competitive on the world market. The designers, most of whom were still wedded to handcraft, would work with German industries to raise the quality of their products. The Werkbund then, in its original incarnation, was less an artistic movement than a state-sponsored attempt to integrate traditional crafts and industrial mass-production technologies. Loos saw something else. It was yet another bid, he thought, to "reform" the crafts and make them more modern.

The first effort to do so, Loos argues, had failed utterly. The endeavor around the turn of the century to introduce the new "art" (i.e., the Jugendstil) into handcraft, he claimed, had produced laughable results: "The inkwells (a rock ledge with two nymphs), the candlesticks (a girl holding a jug, with a candle sticking in it), the furniture (the bedside tables are small drums, the sideboard a large drum with a fretwork oak tree surrounding it) remained unsold. And those who did buy them were ashamed of them two years later."[6]

Loos's assessment of what happened next is brutally funny (at the expense of nearly every other designer working at the time): Those who had made these monstrosities "got nowhere with art. But they were now part of the scene and had to make a living. And so, they hit on a way out [of their predicament]: to help culture find its legs."

At this point, Loos's argument becomes more opaque. To get at his full meaning here, we must revisit his ideas about craftspeople. Loos, the son of a stonemason, whose faith in the intentions of honest producers of handcrafts was complete, believed that it was those consummate "makers," not designers or artists, who best understood what was current, what was inherently "modern." To grasp what was genuine about men's fashions, for example, one only had to look at the suits made by the best master tailors. These men understood, in the way that university-trained designers or artists never could, what was truly au courant. They could do so because they shared a collective sense of what was new and "correct." They were the very font of a modern "Kunstwollen," to twist slightly Alois Riegl's term.[7] Modernity was, in Loos's view, a direct outcome of current craft production. This is precisely why "individual" designers could never forge a valid modern culture.

Returning to "Die Überflüssigen," Loos writes: "A common culture—and that is the only kind there is—creates common forms. But the forms of [Henry] Van De Velde's [sic] furniture differ considerably from those of Josef Hoffmann. Which culture should the German choose? The culture of Hoffmann or that of Van de Velde? For that of [Richard] Riemerschmid or [Joseph Maria] Olbrich?"[8]

Loos does not stop there. He insists that these "modern designers" are superfluous, since the process of forging a new modern culture is already taking place in the crafts, without their aid or expertise:

> All crafts that have so far managed to keep these superfluous figures out of their workshops are working at the apex of their powers. The products of these crafts are the only ones that represent the style of our age. They are so much the style of our age that—and this is the only criterion—we do not see them as being in a "style." They are at one with our thoughts and feelings. Our carriages, our glasses, our optical instruments, our umbrellas and walking sticks, our luggage and saddlery, our silver cigarette cases and ornaments,[9] our jewelry, and our clothes are modern. They are modern because thus far none of these unqualified people have assumed positions of authority in these workshops.[10]

If we distill Loos's comments further, he is saying that the culture is evolving regardless of efforts to devise a modern style—that modern style is already present in the works of good craftspeople. It need not be "invented."

In "Ornament und Verbrechen" (Ornament and Crime), certainly the best known of Loos's essays, he takes this argument further. Loos wrote the piece in late 1909 or early 1910 in response to the ongoing debate in the German-speaking orbit about whether ornament had a place in the modern world.[11] Loos was not the only one at the time to suggest that ornament broadly speaking was now passé. But it is only by referring to his larger cultural argument that the true meaning of his statements become fully apparent.

Once more, Loos attacks those who are seeking to contrive a modern style. He singles out designers like Olbrich, Otto Eckmann, and Van de Velde—along with Hoffmann, his perpetual bête noire—because their efforts to make modern ornament fly in the face of reality: modernism, he states again, is happening on its own—nonetheless. In the only italicized sentence in the piece, he issues a summary of his views, in the standard translation: *"the evolution of culture is synonymous with the removal of ornament from objects of daily use."*[12]

Two words stand out here. The first is "removal." The German word Loos uses is *entfernen*. It can imply an active process—to deliberately clear something away, for example. But the word has another, slightly different meaning; namely, that something might merely "go away," in a passive sense. Thus, a better translation would be "disappear." This is, I believe, is how Loos intended the sentence to read. The whole phrase then should be: "the evolution of culture is synonymous with the disappearance of ornament from objects of daily use." Loos is saying that ornament is withering away because it is no longer necessary, important, or appropriate. It is simply happening—no agency (or agent) is required.

The second, for which there is no single word in English, is *gebrauchsgegenstand* (here not capitalized, as would be customary in German, because Loos rejected the practice of capitalizing all nouns in his later writings). "Objects of daily use" is the usual translation. It is important to state, though, precisely what Loos means. *Gebrauchsgegenstände* are those articles we use in the course of our daily lives. A comb, for example, or a pot or pan in the kitchen. Loos is using the term to draw a very important distinction for him, between those objects that are not part of our quotidian existence—art, monuments, monumental buildings, etc.—and everyday things. The evolution of culture, he contends, is leading toward the disappearance of ornament from everyday objects. No designer is necessary; change is taking place of its own accord—*nonetheless*.

Loos goes on to write that "no one, not even the power of the state, can arrest the evolution of mankind. It can only be slowed down."[13] What he does not say—despite the statements of many observers to the contrary—is that ornament is a crime per se, or that all ornament should be systematically banished.

With regard to the first of these statements, the making of ornament is the equivalent of a crime, Loos doesn't mean that literally, or not quite. If one reads the piece with care, it is evident that Loos is suggesting—satirically—that those who "design" ornament for objects of daily use are like those criminals who tattoo themselves, which for Loos (in an age before the vogue for body art) was a deeply antisocial act. Ornament is only a crime in the economic sense because it costs those who are forced to make it (craftspeople) time and labor, for which they are not compensated properly. "Ornament," he writes, "is wasted labor."[14]

Similarly, Loos is not contending that all ornament should be systematically banished. If one reads the full body of Loos's writings, it is abundantly clear that he believes that ornament still has a place in art and in important buildings and monuments—any object or structure that should say something. Art symbolizes and speaks to us of important matters. An object of daily use does not have this requirement. Loos does admit that ornament can still give us pleasure, even when it is not associated with a work of art. "I can accept the African's ornament, the Persian's, the Slovak peasant woman's, my shoemaker's, for it provides the high point of their existence."[15] Older forms of ornament, in his view, still retain their validity.

But Loos, always the keen observer, recognizes something else: that the pace of evolution is different in different places and different cultures. On the one hand, he condemns the "stragglers." Yet he also leaves an out for those who, by dint of where and how they live, such as peasants in the countryside, haven't yet reached the same level of development. Thus, it is socially acceptable, for instance, for the Papuan in New Guinea to kill and eat his enemies, but not for an "advanced" European.

Today, we can see this argument for what it is: deeply Eurocentric and culturally biased. Loos writes about those "aristocrats"—white, urban-dwelling Europeans—who are at "the peak of humanity": "A modern person, who regards ornament as a symptom of the artistic superfluity of previous ages and for that reason holds it sacred, will immediately recognize the unhealthy, the forced—

painfully forced—nature of modern ornament."[16] This does not take away from Loos's understanding of cultural evolution. He sees with a sparkling lucidity that the world, his world, is changing very rapidly, and that change has little to do with individual will. Modernization, and with it, modernism, was instead a collective reaction to the ways in which industrialization, urbanization, and other forces of change were impacting everyday life. Loos's response is to accept that change, while holding onto practices and objects that still had meaning or relevance. No other course of action makes sense because this change is happening, *nonetheless*.

Yet Loos inserts an important corrective in "Ornament and Crime." He sees the inexorability of change, but he also detects the fact that change, even in modern times, is measured, and that not every design form is destined to become "extinct." In the second of his "formulas," he states, "The form of an object should last, that is, we should find it tolerable as long as the object itself lasts."[17] Fashion, Loos concedes, changes quickly, but other objects, especially well-made objects, will hold their value. Their forms will remain valid over time—until the objects wears out or loses its purpose.

Loos summarizes these views most completely in another of his essays. It is the least read of the three I have included here. Still, it is perhaps the most important for our discussion and for understanding Loos's views on ornament more generally.

He titled it "Ornament und Erziehung" (Ornament and Education). He did not write the piece as an essay. It began instead as a response to a survey sent out by František Viktor Mokrý, a noted Prague painter, graphic designer, pedagogue, and theoretician, asking prominent figures about the present and future course of arts education.[17] Mokrý was the editor of the Czech-language journal *Náš směr* (Our Direction), which examined, among other issues relating to contemporary art, the question of aesthetic education. Loos responded to the survey in German, but it was originally published in the journal in 1924, in Czech translation.[19] Loos later republished the essay in the original German in *Trotzdem*, along with the letter he wrote to Mokrý when he returned the survey.[20]

The piece is arranged as a set of general questions (from Mokrý), with Loos's responses. To the question "Do modern people need ornament?," Loos answers, in part: "Modern people, people with modern nerves, do not need ornament. On the contrary, they abhor it. All objects we call modern do not have ornament." And he is equally adamant that architects or designers should not make new ornament: "Individuals—and that therefore includes architects—are incapable of creating a new form. . . . Form and ornament are products of the subconscious collaboration of all members of a particular culture."

In response to the second of Mokrý's questions, "Should ornament, as an expression of a lack of culture, be eliminated from the world in general, and especially from schools?," Loos gives perhaps his most pointed answer to the problem of cultural evolution. He says, unambiguously, "Ornament will disappear on its own accord, and schools should not interfere in this natural process, which humanity has been going through ever since it came into existence."[21]

To this, he adds:

> Twenty-six years ago [*sic*][22] I claimed that the use of ornamentation on objects of practical use would disappear with the development of mankind, a constant and consistent development, which was as natural a process as the atrophying of vowels in the final syllables in popular speech. By that I did not mean what some purists have insisted *ad absurdum*, namely that ornament should be systematically and consistently eliminated. What I did mean was that where it had disappeared as an indispensable consequence of human development, it could not be restored, just as people will never return to tattooing their faces.[23]

If Loos's prediction about tattooing was faulty, his explication of cultural evolution rings true. Change happens. Change happens over time. Cultural evolution is broadly based—it is the result of collective, not individual, action. And cultural evolution never entails "wholesale rejection." Some vestiges of the past will remain—those that continue to be useful or speak to us about our past (in the form of nostalgia).

Armed with this knowledge, it becomes much easier to "read" Loos's architecture, especially his interiors, for they represent a set of choices or prescriptions issuing from his ideas about the process of cultural evolution. Two examples may suffice.

In the Albertina's Loos Archive is a particularly lovely photograph of Loos and his first wife, Lina, sitting in their new, not yet fully furnished apartment on the Bösendorferstraße (fig. 1.2). To their backs is a hearth, and visible also are the beamed ceilings and two built-in cabinets. One reading would be that Loos's design is making direct reference to the English Arts and Crafts movement and

| 1.2. Loos and his first wife, Lina, enjoying the first fire in their new apartment on the Bösendorferstraße, 1903. Adolf Loos Archiv, Albertina, Vienna, ALA 2388.

to English vernacular interiors. That is unquestionably correct. But there is more. Loos's design is also speaking about the persistence and modernity of craft and craftsmanship on the part of the masons who laid the fireplace; the metalworkers who cut, hammered, and bent the hood; and cabinetmakers, who supplied the built-ins and beams. And he is referencing another of his ideas—that objects from the past can still be viable.

This is even more poignantly spelled out in Loos's dining room in the Steiner House, which he installed in 1910 (fig. 1.3). The same warm, cottagey look is present. Each piece of furniture or object is part of his rigorous process of reading through a cultural lens. Some of the objects are there because they

| 1.3. Adolf Loos, House for Hugo and Lily Steiner, Vienna, 1910, dining space. Adolf Loos Archiv, Albertina, Vienna, ALA 3240.

represent "readymades" (to recast Duchamp's concept). These are pieces from the past that are consummate examples of design or craftsmanship (or really both) and that retain their worth. The Oriental carpet, for instance—a piece presenting old ornament that can still give us joy; or the Chippendale chairs, which retain their gracefulness and comfort. Other objects, like the sideboard, are Loos's designs: they fuse the past and present, quietly, in the way that a good cabinetmaker might. And, finally, there are the silver and porcelain pieces: bowls, candlesticks, and the like, which were presumably heirlooms from the Steiners' families. For Loos, such objects have a place in modern interiors because they are reminders of the past—of people and events; they need not be cast off but treasured and passed on.

It is all consistent with his views. Loos's design outlook, his own distinctive aesthetic, and his very idea of what constitutes modernism stem from his beliefs about the nature of cultural evolution. It all comes about "nonetheless."

Plate Number 196

2 | The Iconic Tower

What is there left to be said about Adolf Loos's entry to the *Chicago Tribune* competition in 1922, his great Doric column that was to have been built of gleaming black granite (fig. 2.1)? Katherine Solomonson, who wrote the definitive account of the competition, presents a full laundry list of reactions: "Seen variously as a joke, a caustic critique, and a sophisticated essay rich in metaphorical allusions, Loos's column," she writes, "has triggered wide-ranging interpretations: it expresses the *Tribune's* growth and power, as it did that of the Roman Empire; it playfully alludes to a newspaper's printed columns; it refers to the columnar metaphor describing the skyscraper's tripartite division; it takes a critical stand against the American city; it is Dada, it is ironic, it is utterly empty of meaning."[1] To that list, we can add Anthony Vidler, who famously remarked of Loos and his intentions that he "is always serious but never deadly so."[2] Then there is Benedetto Gravagnuolo, who called Loos's classical column "an out-of-date object drawn from historical memory."[3]

|2.1. Adolf Loos, project for the *Chicago Tribune* competition tower. From *The International Competition for a New Administration Building for the Chicago Tribune MCXXII* (Chicago: Tribune Company, 1923), plate 196.

It is easy to make such assertions, far more difficult to establish their validity. And with a project so peculiar and so fraught, the challenge is that much greater. So much of what has been written about Loos and the tower does not bear up, even under gentle scrutiny. What does it mean, for example, to say that Loos took "a critical stand against the American city?" Where in Loos's writings does he pick up this theme? The evidence, scant though it is, points to the opposite. Loos, from all we know, was deeply enamored of the new American skyscrapers: in his papers, for example, are several postcards of tall buildings in Chicago. Some, if not all, we know he collected after his time in America. How exactly is his tower a "critique"?

Then there is the assertion that the tower is "Dada." The Dadaists famously rejected the mores and logic of bourgeois society; their response came in the form of nonsense and irrationality. Loos's great tower, eccentric as it may be, is not nonsensical. Quite the contrary. And if Loos was sometimes critical of European middle-class taste, he was no Dadaist (even if he would later build a house for one, Tristan Tzara).

Statements like these have a certain superficial attraction, but they are devoid of substance. Is the tower truly empty of meaning? Loos surely meant what he said, even if at times he overstated it—and the notion that he would make a building, especially a large, monumental building, lacking entirely in meaning, flies in the face of everything that he wrote about buildings, monumentality, and art. There is no doubt that Loos cared profoundly about his work; he cared about his buildings' usefulness and how they would fulfill their cultural role. He was convinced, to his very last days, that his approach (and very often, his approach alone) was right and fitting. I have no idea what it means to say, as Vidler does, that Loos was never "deadly serious." Loos made many unrealized projects, in some instances when there was no realistic chance that they might be carried out. But he always presented solutions that spoke directly about what a particular building was and what it should mean. He made jokes, but only little ones.

Still, glib commentary aside, the question of what Loos intended persists. If one is to say something meaningful, it is best to start with what we do know.

There are hints in the actual contemporary texts and drawings that relate to the *Chicago Tribune* project, but one of the powerful testimonials comes in the account that Loos's second wife, Elsie Altmann-Loos, wrote in her later years.[4]

Elsie was married to Loos at the time of the competition; she presents us with a detailed description of his work on the *Tribune* tower. Like much else in her book, the tale she relates is at once wrenching and revealing. She wrote her book from memory—many years after her marriage to Loos had ended in divorce. She was then living half a world away, in Buenos Aires, Argentina, where she had found refuge after the rise of the Nazis. If one reads the book with a judicious eye and compares her narrative with what we know about Loos's life and work, it becomes clear that she not infrequently misremembered or misread events. In this instance, though, Elsie's recounting has the sturdy ring of truth. What it says runs counter to very much of what has been written about Loos and his remarkable tower project. "Loos," she writes,

> designed an enormous Doric column, looking rather like how one might imagine the Tower of Babel. It was truly an extraordinary project. Loos worked for many months on the concept. [Heinrich] Kulka and [Leopold] Fischer assisted him. The final days were awful, for the drawings had to be sent off on a certain ship, in order to arrive in Chicago at the right time. Kulka and Fischer worked in our apartment like men completely obsessed, and in the final days I even helped to ink the drawings and pack them. The only one who showed no hint of hurry and who practically held up the work, was Loos. I had a vague feeling that he somehow wanted the shipment of the drawings to be delayed, because he must have sensed that the first prize could only go to an American. Loos, by the way, was not the only European architect who took part in the competition—there were at least two others.[5] As it happened, the drawings of his project arrived too late, and he was not considered for the prize. The prize instead went to an American architect for a rather mediocre design. Which is not saying anything new.[6]

Elsie may have been correct when she suggests that Loos had delayed sending the competition entry because he was trying to shield himself from rejection. That is not entirely clear. What she adds to her account, though, exposes a different side of Loos and his ambitions:

> What no one knows is the following story: When Loos and I were spending time in Nice in 1923—it must have been around February—Loos read in an English-language newspaper that Mr. [Robert R.] McCormick [the *Chicago Tribune*'s co-owner and co-editor], who was staying in Monte Carlo, was planning to attend a party in Cannes and would travel on the

> *Train Bleu*. The *Bleu* in those days was a super luxury train, and it was undoubtedly nicer to go by that train than by automobile.
>
> On this particular day, Loos left early for Monte Carlo and purchased a ticket there for the *Train Bleu* to Nice. He was convinced that in the brief hour that the train needed to go from Monte Carlo to Nice, he could win Mr. McCormick's sympathy and understanding. He wanted to explain that his project had not arrived before the deadline and to ask him to study it closely, because [Mr. McCormick] had not seen it. He was sure that Mr. McCormick would forgive everything, and he would appreciate his genial idea [for the building] and the necessity of catching Mr. McCormick on the *Train Bleu*, because he certainly would not have received Loos in his hotel.[7]

It says much that Loos took the effort—and the risk—of confronting McCormick on the train. His actions suggest a deep desire to see his building realized; they also reveal his conviction—however naive or misguided—that he could hastily persuade McCormick of the rightness of his idea and win the day.

In the end, it all went terribly wrong. Loos did meet McCormick, who was in the company of two other men. McCormick, as Elsie describes, was "visibility impatient" with Loos when he broke into their conversation, and he expressed his annoyance. Loos's attempts to persuade the American that building his design would be a "world event" served only to further irritate him. Elsie's description of Loos's action that night is especially poignant: "Loos verteidigte sein Geschöpf, das Projekt, wie eine Mutter ihr Kind" (Loos defended his creature, his project, like a mother defending her child).[8] Despite (or, more likely, because of) Loos's fervent pleadings, "McCormick requested not very politely that Loos leave his compartment and not to bother him anymore."[9]

Loos returned to the couple's hotel room visibly shaken and silent. He went to bed without eating. Elsie, who often knew just the right thing to say to placate her husband even in his bleakest moments, persuaded him that McCormick must have been drunk; otherwise, he would not have behaved as he had. Loos accepted her interpretation, and "the matter was never mentioned again."[10]

It is a charming tale in some ways. That Loos would have come up with a scheme to meet McCormick and convince him of the rightness of building *his* design, rather than the winning entry, sounds like something out of a contemporary novel, maybe one written by Anita Loos (no relation), the American starlet and screenwriter best known for her 1925 comic novel *Gentlemen Prefer Blondes*. The scene on the train reminds one of the madcap moments in her stories. There is a strong aroma of naiveté in Loos's actions. Did he truly believe that he could induce a seasoned and hard-nosed businessman like McCormick to change the outcome of a widely publicized competition in the course of a short train ride? Apparently, if we are to believe Elsie, he did. It borders on the silly—or the pathetic.

Loos, we know from other testimonials, could at times be childlike or wholly deluded, living in his own fantasy world. Claire Beck Loos, Loos's last wife, in her memoir of her time with him, writes of how he spent days looking for property along the Riviera to build on, even though he had no client and no money of his own. When she confronts him about the unreality of it all, his response surprises her: "He looks at me disappointed. Defiant, like a child who is about to have his favorite toy taken away, he replies: 'How could you spoil the enjoyment I am getting from working on this project by asking that, Lerle! [his nickname for her]. Didn't I tell you we have to be ready for when the rich financier shows up?!' Irritated, he leaves me; soon he has rebuilt the entire Riviera in his head."[11]

Still, Loos's actions on the train, and his dejection afterward, suggest that he very much wanted to build his great tower. There is no indication here that his proposal was a joke or a game.

We know only a little about the genesis of Loos's project. According to Elsie, he worked on the concept for "many months." He (and his assistants), however, apparently only began working in earnest on the final drawings a short time before the deadline. The first call "to build a monument of enduring beauty" went out in the *Chicago Tribune* on June 10, 1922.[12] Loos would have learned about it soon thereafter. The information about the competition was disseminated internationally through an extensive network of newspapers and professional publications.[13]

Entries had to be postmarked by November 1 to be considered.[14] That meant that Loos had fewer than four months to complete and submit a design. The only evidence we have for his design process beyond what Elsie tells us is in a few remaining drawings in the Loos Archive housed in the Albertina Museum in Vienna. The drawings are not dated, so it is impossible to say when he might have begun the work, or how long he took to complete it. We do know that it was Loos's habit to *think* about his designs for some time before he committed pencil to paper. He was not an architect who habitually sat at the drafting table sketching out different possibilities. Especially in his later years, Loos, as his various assistants have testified, first conceived of what he wanted in his head—often down to very small details—before making any sort of drawing. Those drawings were usually rudimentary, at best. He would then hand his sketch or sketches over to an assistant, along with extensive verbal instructions. If Loos held form in this instance, he may not have produced any drawings at all until shortly before the deadline.

What appears to be the earliest drawing is an undated pencil sketch of several variant towers (fig. 2.2). The two smaller ones on the lower right look like building envelope studies. Perhaps Loos was thinking first of the form before he considered the question of architectonic language. In any event, the two larger towers suggest that he was thinking about using the cloak of a purified classicism almost from the outset. The blocky tower, pilaster-like, on the left is the more conventional solution. It followed Louis Sullivan's dictum that a tall building should replicate the standard classical tripartite division of base, body, and cap. The overall look is columnar. Here, though, the massive structure has been transformed with the addition of regular fenestration. And next to this first "column" is a second one, a Greek Doric one, which has not yet been "converted" into a building. Loos's final tower proposal was a melding of these two: the Doric column made into a habitable tower.

This early drawing also shows one other important feature of the building: its large, stair-stepped base. Doric columns originally did not have bases; the columns rested directly on a stylobate. Doric columns with bases first began appearing in the Hellenistic period, but it was only later, during Roman times, that such bases became more common. Often these were stair-stepped, but the specific form Loos applied here seems to have come from his own stock of ideas: the lower tower block recalls the unrealized mausoleum he designed for the Czech-born architectural historian and preservationist Max Dvořák in 1921 (fig. 2.3).

The original plans called for the Dvořák vault to be erected in Vienna's Zentralfriedhof, with interior frescoes painted by Oskar Kokoschka.[14] In the end, Dvořák was interred in a conventional grave on the estate of Prince Franz Liechtenstein in Hrušovany near Znojmo. Loos may have reused the form, albeit elongated and at much larger scale. But this matters little; similar stair-stepped massing appears often in Loos's work—before and after the *Tribune* design—and often enough that it was almost a signature form for him.

|2.2. Adolf Loos, alternative tower designs for the *Chicago Tribune* competition tower, perspectives. Pencil on paper. Adolf Loos Archiv, Albertina, Vienna, ALA 683.

|2.3. Adolf Loos, Mausoleum for Max Dvořák, model, 1921. Adolf Loos Archiv, Albertina, Vienna, ALA 2184.

Loos apparently continued to refine his idea. The first full iteration of his giant Doric column on a stair-stepped base is probably the one shown in a faint pencil drawing in the Albertina (fig. 2.4). In this rendering, the tower is massive, as is the ten-story base. A pair of enormous Doric columns, three stories high, frame either side of the main entrance in an arrangement that recalls Loos's earliest design for the Goldman & Salatsch building on Michaelerplatz (1909–11). At some point after that, Loos had an assistant (Kulka or Fischer, or perhaps both) make a large-scale presentation drawing of this design (fig. 2.5). And, possibly later, Loos and his assistants also worked on a sketch of the building's ground floor and a lower floor in the base (Adolf Loos Archiv, Albertina, Vienna [hereafter ALA], 310).

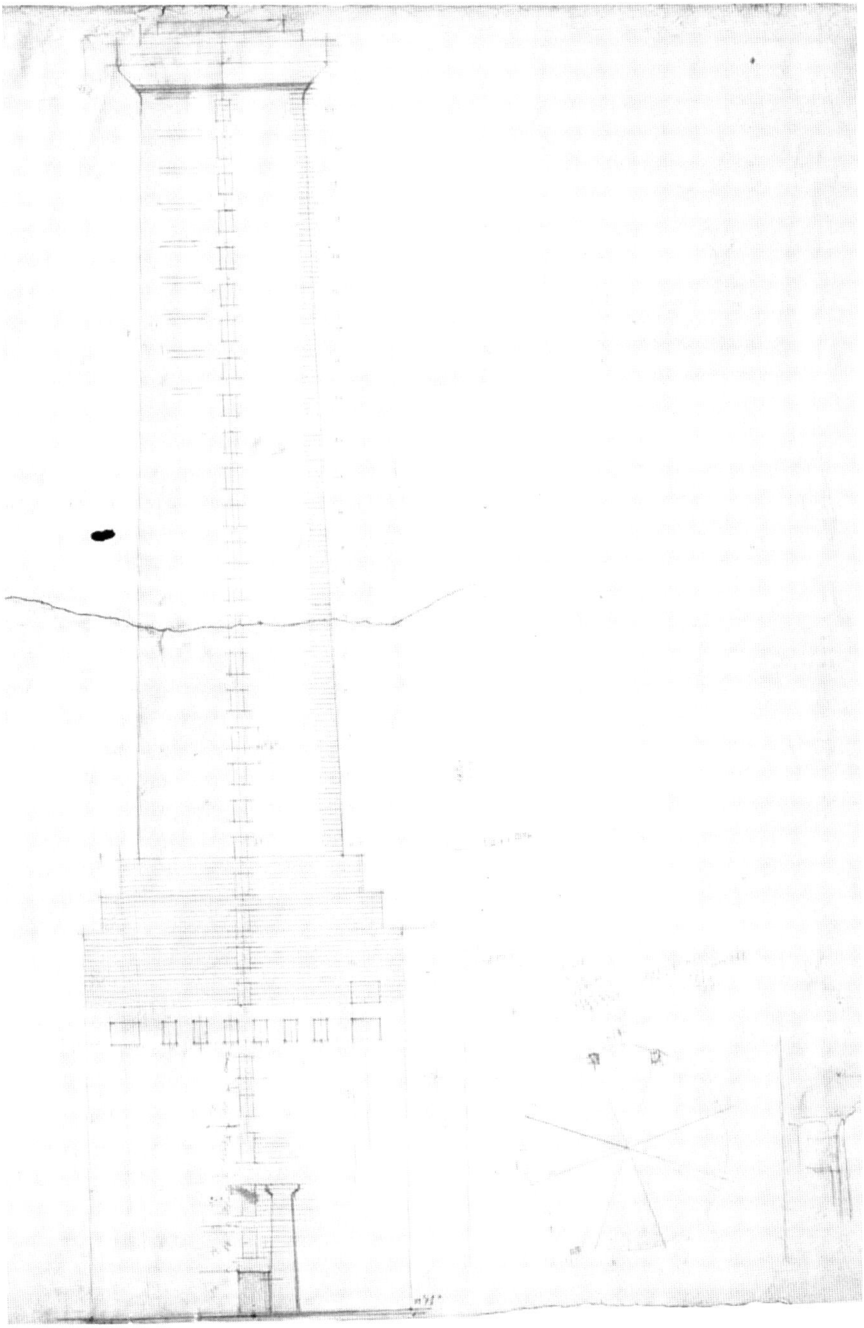

|2.4. Adolf Loos, project for the *Chicago Tribune* competition tower, elevation. Pencil on paper. Adolf Loos Archiv, Albertina, Vienna, ALA 310.

Loos must have been dissatisfied with the result, because he substantially reworked the design. He altered the base, adding one additional story (making it eleven floors rather than ten), resulting in a whole that was slightly taller and more attenuated. He also changed the form of the two columns flanking the entry. In the last version, they are broader at the base and taper dramatically inward near the top; their capitals are also larger and more affected. And to lend greater weightiness, they are shown as huge, monolithic blocks of stone, rather than the "composite" columns in the earlier version, made up of smaller ashlar stone units.

The most notable difference, however, is in the tower itself. Loos thinned it, introducing a characteristic bulge at the center (i.e., employing entasis, the conventional "optical" correction of the Greek architects), and he recast the top, making an abacus (the block portion of the capital), which is larger and more impressive than the "ring" arrangement of the intermediate version (fig. 2.6). The result was a soaring tower with an impressive entrance, framed by muscular, monolithic columns and a mighty top, constituted as if it were supporting the sky itself.

And Loos made one more significant change. In the initial design, the one with the shorter base, the shaft of the column is smooth. The final version shows the shaft of the column, which is to say the main body of the tower, as fluted, giving it a strong vertical emphasis. It is every bit the proud, soaring structure Sullivan had championed. Whether or not Loos took this from other American skyscrapers (such as the Woolworth Building, with its insistent verticality) is uncertain, but the effect would have been striking.

Would Loos genuinely have taken such efforts if the project were intended as a "joke" or a "meaningless" or "empty" gesture?

There is at least one aspect of the design that *is* comical, though not, I think, intentionally so: his section drawing of a typical tower floor (fig. 2.7). The spatial divisions are crude, and the addition of the legend that indicates the "pipes" looks rather silly now. Still, Loos, one has to say, was working with an unfamiliar form; inhabitable round structures are comparatively rare in architecture. He (or his assistants) did their best to suggest how the tower might be made into usable spaces.

|2.5. Adolf Loos, project for the *Chicago Tribune* competition tower, elevation. Pencil on paper. Adolf Loos Archiv, Albertina, Vienna, ALA 221.

·THE CHICAGO TRIBVNE COLVMN·

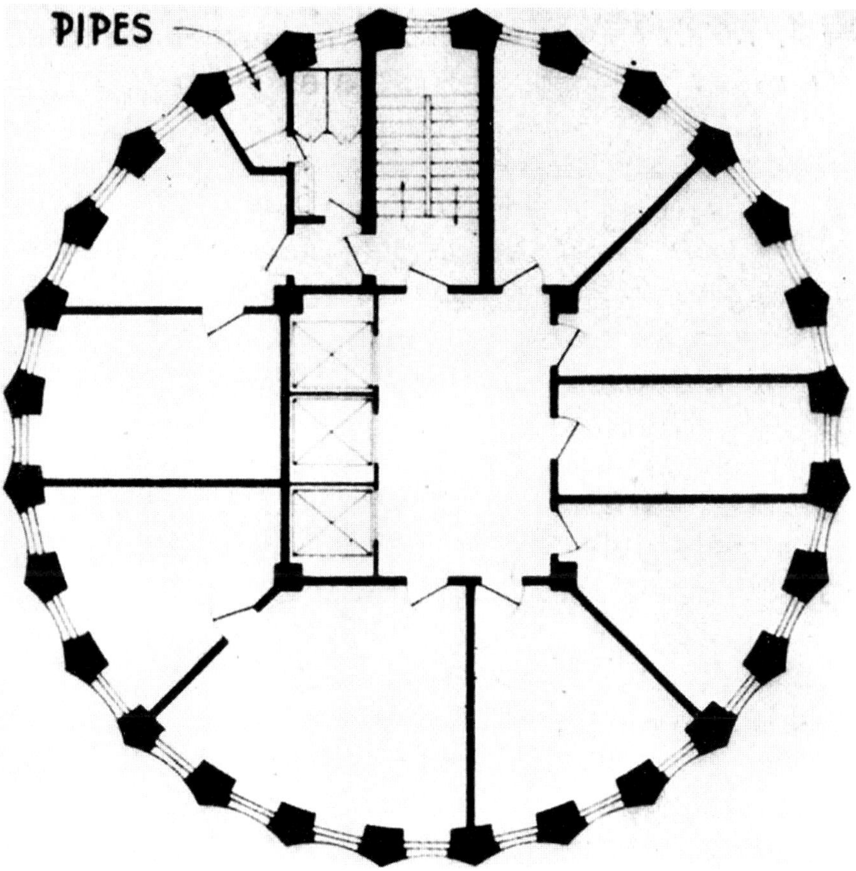

|2.7. Adolf Loos, plan of a typical tower floor, project for the *Chicago Tribune* competition tower. Pencil on paper. Adolf Loos Archiv, Albertina, Vienna, ALA 310.

|2.6. Adolf Loos, presentation drawing for the *Chicago Tribune* competition tower, elevation. Pencil on paper. Adolf Loos Archiv, Albertina, Vienna, ALA 378.

But the central questions remain. Why a classical conceit? Why specifically a Doric column? What were Loos's true intentions?

Gravagnuolo, writing at the time when postmodernism was in its ascendancy, sees Loos's recourse to antiquity as part of his propensity to play "language games." He argues that Loos was only following the technique of "linguistic montage tried out by the great Viennese master" Fischer von Erlach, "who introduced the eclectic revival of the great linguistic repertory of classical antiquity to Viennese architectural culture."[16] Gravagnuolo specifically cites the example of the Karlskirche, the Church of St. Charles Borromeo, with its multiple classical allusions, including its Pantheon-like portico and its twin towers that borrow directly from Trajan's Column. That fact that Loos's apartment on the Bösendorferstraße was only a few hundred meters away seemingly bolsters the argument. But Loos knew well the practice of quotation in Western architecture: he did not need Fischer's church to remind him of it. And he was hardly alone as a modernist in quoting from the past. All the early modern masters were steeped in architectural history; most quoted from it in some fashion, though usually less directly. Le Corbusier and Ludwig Mies van der Rohe indeed were and remained in some measure "crypto-classicists."[17]

It is Loos's direct citation that stands out. Gravagnuolo sees the essence of what Loos is doing in his propensity for basic forms:

> Apart from his game of learned quotations, there is a desire in Loos to go back to the essential purity of archaic forms. It is no coincidence that the stepped pyramid will be used again for the compositional layout of the large Department Store in Alexandria (1910), for the Grand Hotel Babylon (1923), for the Mausoleum of Max Dvořák (1921) and yet again for the base of the Chicago Tribune Column (1922). Thus architecture on the drawing board plays a fundamental role in Loos' design strategy; it represents an ideal laboratory for research into elements of language that may be reused, on a larger or smaller scale, in the diverse expressions of an essentially unitary process.[18]

Here, I think, Gravagnuolo is much closer to the mark. The notion of a purified classicism *is* decidedly at play in Loos's design. Loos is certainly making recourse to an earlier form in an effort to look back to the origins of Western architecture—a quest that was widely shared by the early Viennese modernists.

Others, including Ludwig Münz, who wrote extensively about Loos and had a central part in publishing his writings, and Eduard F. Sekler, who was the biographer of Josef Hoffmann, have pointed to a possible source: Loos's supposed interest in the Bunker Hill Monument (1825–43) in Boston, which is in the form of a massive obelisk (fig. 2.8).[19] Loos kept a treasured postcard of it, and it may have been the inspiration for several of his designs, including the church tower he designed in 1899 to commemorate the Emperor Franz Joseph's jubilee.[20]

|2.8. Solomon Willard, Bunker Hill Monument, Boston, Massachusetts, 1825–43. Photograph: Detroit Publishing Co., New York, 1890–1901. Library of Congress, Prints and Photographs Division, Washington, D.C.

The Bunker Hill Monument, designed by a man named Solomon Willard, a carver and builder known for some of the classical details he contributed to Boston's early buildings and little else, fulfills the role of a pure, archaic form. Loos does seem to have had a certain fascination with it. Perhaps it was the way in which the scale was altered while the form remained unchanged, which was exactly Loos's strategy in the *Tribune* proposal. But, of course, the Bunker Hill Monument is not habitable, and to make it habitable would have greatly undermined its purity as an object.

Another rather interesting suggestion for the source of Loos's idea comes from American art historian Joseph Masheck. He too alludes to the Bunker Hill Monument as a possible model for the Chicago tower, but he goes a step further. Masheck, following Sekler, submits that Loos may have been influenced by the American sculptor and theorist Horatio Greenough (1805–52), who was one of the "instigators" of the Bunker Hill Monument and an early opponent of ornament. Masheck writes: "It is not farfetched to think of Loos having been influenced by the architectural texts of Greenough, whose own tracts against architectural ornament were to be rediscovered during the heyday of postwar 'functionalism' in American architecture and design."[21] The problem with linking Loos with Greenough, though, is exactly what Masheck writes: that he was only rediscovered much later. Greenough was not widely read when Loos was in America or during the two and half decades afterward; I think it is unlikely that Loos would have encountered his ideas, either directly or indirectly.

Masheck also points to another possible source, "the more contemporaneous architectural polemics of Louis Sullivan." Masheck alludes to a specific text of Sullivan's, "A Doric Column," which was published in Sullivan's posthumous book *Kindergarten Chats*. The piece, as he writes,

> concerns a, to Sullivan, absurd proposal to memorialize the bicentennial of Detroit with the world's largest monumental Doric column. Taking the idea as fatuous, Sullivan treats it wryly enough to have delighted Loos, several times referring, in mock-deference to the diction of illiterate rubes, to "the architek" (*sic*; Sullivan, *Kindergarten Chats* [58–60]). Moreover, in the essay "On Scholarship" (chapter xl), in the same collection, Sullivan writes: "When we ask an architect to build a memorial to the Great Lakes, the primeval forests and the hardy *voyageurs*—and he gives us a Doric Column, he is not a scholar, he is a faker! So, when we ask an architect to build a twenty-odd story office-building, and he

> throws up a swaggering mass of Roman remnants, he is not a scholar but a brute."[22]

If Loos were making a joke with his tower, if he intended it as a bold ironic gesture, this is a splendid bit of evidence. If true, it explains everything: Loos was not serious; he was giving the American "rubes" what he thought they deserved.

There are two major problems with this idea. First, we do not know whether Loos read the piece; he makes no mention of it anywhere in his own writings. If he did design his building in accord with Sullivan's assertions, it seems odd that Loos would never have referred to this passage. Even more to the point, Masheck assumes that Loos was in agreement with Sullivan, which is assuming a great deal. Loos admired Sullivan. Of that there is no doubt. But he cannot but have been troubled by Sullivan's "ornamentalist" stance. Sullivan made remarkable ornament; Loos abhorred modern ornament. One cannot say that any more clearly. Moreover, Loos's views about classicism and its meanings—especially its relevance for the present—stood in direct opposition to Sullivan's. The whole idea that Loos would have seized on this text as a guide for his project appears rather improbable.

Masheck also makes mention of another fact: that Loos had a decided advantage over most of the other Europeans who submitted designs. That is unquestionably true. He had been to Chicago, albeit briefly (for approximately a week) in 1893. He had a sense of the city, its setting, and the skyscrapers that had been built there—at least to the time of his visit. But did this influence his design? Was he merely offering the equivalent of an architectural "snide remark" to the city and its urban context?

To make this argument, one has to believe that Loos did not "mean" for his proposal to be taken seriously. But everything in his actions, if Elise is to be believed, suggests otherwise.

There is another powerful piece of evidence concerning Loos's intentions, and it comes in the form of the statement he sent along with his proposal. It was published in January 1923, in the *Zeitschrift des österreichischen Ingenieur- und Architekten-Vereines*.

I reproduce it here, in its entirety, in translation:

> When designing this project, the architect had in mind the program's requirement "to erect the most beautiful and distinctive office building in the world," to build a building that, when viewed only a single time

in a photograph or in reality, can never again be erased from one's memory, to build a monument that will forever be inseparable from the image of the city of Chicago, like the dome of St. Peters in Rome or The Leaning Tower in Pisa, to design a building that will connect all intellectual people with the distinctiveness of *The Chicago Tribune* newspaper.

But how to achieve this goal? To build the tallest building in the world, taller than the Woolworth Building? The height limitation of 400 feet made this impossible. Repeat the trick of the New York Herald or the Morgan Building, by making it lower than the surrounding buildings? It would be impossible to do this and remain true to the spirit of the competition call. Or devise new architectural forms without any connection to tradition, such as those used by the German, Austrian, and French architects who originally came from the cubist Berlin or Belgium of 1848? Alas, these nontraditional forms are all too rapidly supplanted by new ones, and the owner of such a building will soon realize that his building is unfashionable, because these forms are changing like those of ladies' hats.

There might therefore be no other choice than to design a typical American skyscraper, which at the beginning of this phenomenon could easily be distinguished from one another; but nowadays it is difficult for the layman who sees a photo of one of these buildings to discern if it is in San Francisco or Detroit.

The architect of this project decided therefore on a column for his design. There is a long tradition of the free-standing, oversized column: Trajan's Column was the model, for instance, for Napoleon's Column on the Place Vendôme.

Architectural and aesthetic misgivings immediately arose against this idea: Is it permissible to build an inhabited column? In response it must be said that there have never been objections concerning the use of uninhabited monuments for skyscrapers; one might think here of the classic model of the tomb of King Mausolus for the Metropolitan Building and the use of the Gothic steeple for the Woolworth Building.

One can nonetheless rest assured that it will cost me dearly to publish this idea; for what other architects would have no hesitation in doing will not spare me, for I have made a name for myself by relying on the strictest rigor, and I will have to face the reproach of not having remained true to my principles. However, I have not left them, and I vouch fully for my design. I have grown up with close connections to the newspaper business, since I am not only an architect but also a writer and a collaborator with every modern art publication; I worked as a journalist (an art critic) in New York when I was young, I know the limitations of applying architectonic principles to a newspaper building. This design is worthy of the Chicago Tribune; for lesser newspapers it would be pretentious.

Most of the objections will, I fear, be directed at the unadorned nature of my project. My teaching that the ornaments of the ancients should be replaced by noble materials will be expressed here in gigantic form: only one material should be used, black, polished granite.

No graphic representation can describe the full effect of this column; the smooth, polished faces of the cubic base and the fluting of the column would overwhelm the beholder. It would surprise, a sensation, even in our modern and blasé times.

The building is not higher than the regulations allow, but through the perspective effect of the abacus it will appear higher.

I did waste space; every form of monumentality comes at the expense of space: a high entrance hall, a wide stair: the owner should keep in mind that sophistication is not characterized by the cheapest or most expedient means, but that the most impressive effects are achieved through the opposite, as the New York Herald and Morgan buildings prove.

The connection between the main body of the building and the [existing] rear plant shall be of brick and terracotta except for the cornice and the columns, which will be fashioned from the same material as the main building. This is the best way to show that the new building and the existing structure belong together.

> The *Gígantes* above the columns of the entrance correspond best to the Temple of Jupiter in Akragas and the crouching figures of the Theater of Dionysos in Athens.
>
> If the height restriction of 400 feet is removed, a statue of a seated Roman tribune could be placed atop the column. Up to now, large columns have only been erected in the Roman style, never in the Greek. Till now this concept has only been slumbering—now it has found form.
>
> The big Greek Doric column will be built. If not in Chicago, then in another city. If not for the Chicago Tribune, then for someone else. If not by me, then by another architect.[23]

Nothing in this text speaks of a witty riposte to the people of Chicago. Nowhere does Loos suggest that he has anything but respect for the newspaper and the city. There is not even the faintest whiff of mirth or ironic gesture. Loos appears, as I believe he was, entirely sincere about his intentions. The piece is a patient explication of how he came to his design and why he made the choices he did. He refers to some of his models, including, for the *Gígantes* above the entry, the Temple of Jupiter in Akragas (Agrigento) and the Theater of Dionysus in Athens. And he tells us that he specifically chose a Greek Doric form, rather than the Roman one. He even supplies an apologia for "wasting space," something he notes that otherwise was anathema to him, but which he believed was necessary to achieve a monumental effect.

Why should we not take him at his word? The great tower does closely resemble the columns (other than the shafts, which are tapered upward) of several of the temples in Agrigento, including the Temple of Concordia. Loos might have consulted other texts, such as the *Speculum Romanae Magnificentiae*, published in Rome by Antonio Lafreri between 1540 and 1580 (fig. 2.9). He may even have drawn inspiration from the Acropolis itself. Yet the precise source matters little: the design of the shaft and capital display a consummate understanding of the Doric form. Does it not seem unlikely that he would have gone to so much effort to make an ironic gesture?

But, even more, Loos partly answers the question of why he, an architect with a certain reputation as a modernist, would submit such a project: "I have not left [my principles]," he writes, "and I vouch fully for my design."

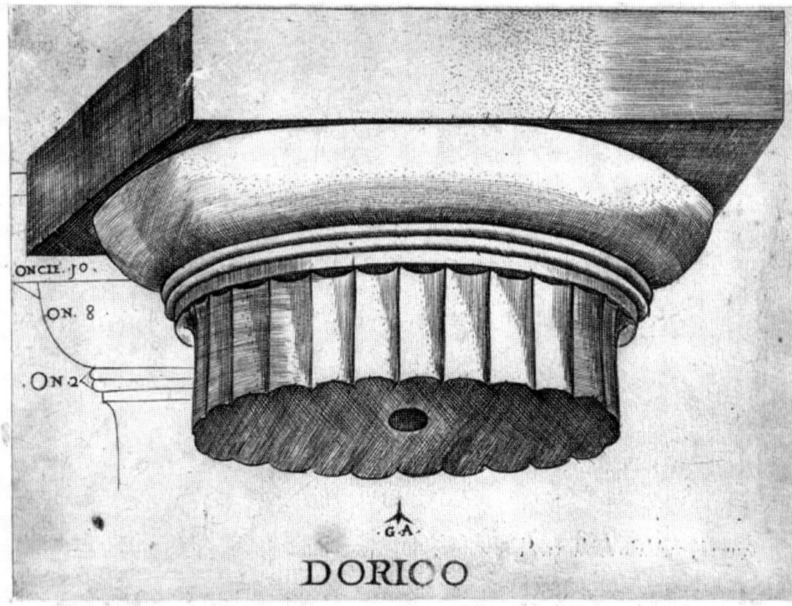

2.9. Detail of a Doric capital, from *Speculum Romanae Magnificentiae*, published in Rome by Antonio Lafreri, ca. 1540–80. Metropolitan Museum of Art, New York, 41.72(1–3).

Despite all this—despite the testimony of Elsie, Loos's own statements, and what we know about Loos and the project—some have remained unconvinced that he was entirely serious about his great Doric tower. Gravagnuolo, for example, writes: "But whatever the biographical data and whatever Loos himself may have said, the Chicago Tribune Column is Dada." His reasoning is twofold: that the tower is a form of "readymade"—a sort of Duchampian thumbing of the nose—and that it was some form of commentary on the city in general and Chicago in particular.[24]

But this argument flies in the face of all that we know about Loos, his ideas, and his practices.

There is a last bit if evidence that I find compelling, and it come to us in Loos's own words. The broader explanation for why Loos resorted to a classical motif is not given in his statement in 1922. It appears instead in 1924, in one of Loos's most important late essays, "Ornament und Erziehung" (Ornament and Education). What he writes about classicism is especially revealing: "Our education is based on classical culture. An architect is a bricklayer who has learned Latin. . . . Classical education has created, despite the differences of languages and frontiers, a common Western culture, to abandon it would be to demolish this last common ground. It is for that reason that we should cultivate not only classical ornament, but also the orders of columns and moldings."[25]

Loos continues, comparing classical ornament to Latin grammar (that "brings discipline to our minds and our souls") and insisting that classical ornament "brings order into the shaping of our objects of everyday use."[26]

Why speak in Latin? Why resort to a past language (even if it were still living) for a modern newspaper building? Why alter the scale of the column so dramatically? Loos never quite tells us. The answer, though, is bound up with what he writes at the end of his description of his design; namely, that he had not abandoned his principles.

The explanation, then (absent any linguistic or discursive games), is clear-cut. Loos rejected the use of modern ornament and the use of any ornament on everyday objects or buildings. He did not do so for monumental buildings or works of art. It was completely appropriate in Loos's mind to "dress" (in the Semperian sense, of cladding the exterior with a stylistic "cloak") an important structure like the *Tribune* building. He wanted to create an icon, and he saw no contradiction in employing an iconic formal language. If the tower now seems like an ironic gesture, it is because it looks ironic to us. To Loos, it appeared entirely logical. He believed fervently in the endurance of classicism and classical imagery. He did not get the joke because he wasn't joking.

I should perhaps add here one more thought about Loos's points of reference and his design process. As I have noted, there has been a long discourse about Loos's purported sources for the *Tribune* tower. The likely suspects include the Bunker Hill Monument, Trajan's Column, and the twin columns of the Vienna Karlskirche. This all makes good sense—up to a point. But none of these structures is designed for habitation. Could Loos have been thinking about another round structure as a model? A possibility is a building Loos would have known well, the so-called Narrenturm (literally, Fool's Tower), or psychiatric hospital, in Vienna, designed by Isidore Canevale and completed in 1784 (fig. 2.10). What is striking is the degree to which the rustication and fenestration of the building resemble Loos's early projects for his tower. And because the building was designed expressly to be inhabited (with 139 individual cells for the inmates), it could have offered a working model for Loos's first version of the shaft of the tower.

|2.10. Isidore Canevale, Narrenturm, Vienna, 1784. Private collection.

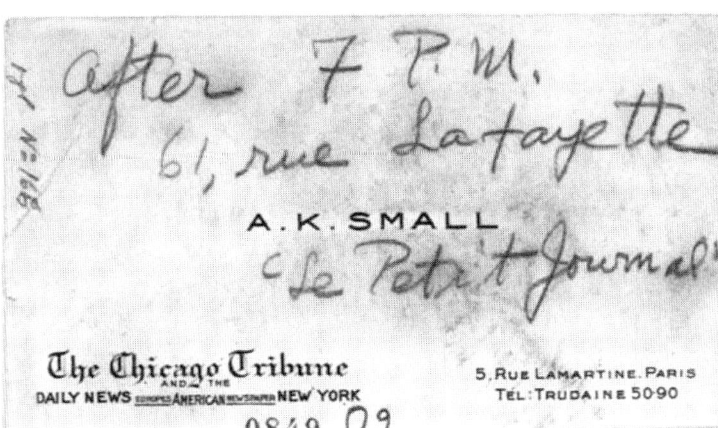

|2.11. Business card of A. K. Small, from the *Chicago Tribune* office in Paris, ca. 1923. Adolf Loos Archiv, Albertina, Vienna, ALA 849v.

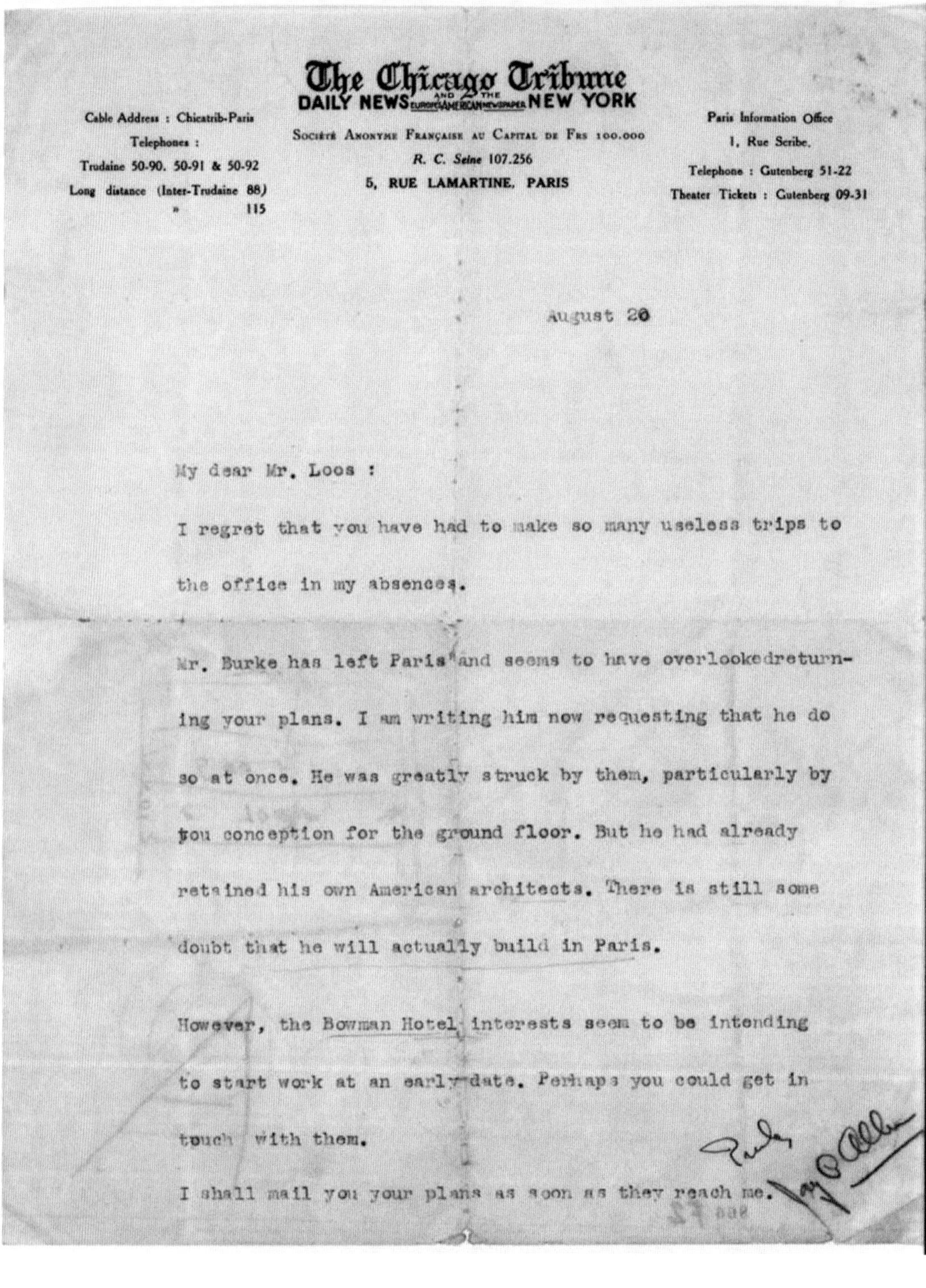

The Chicago Tribune
DAILY NEWS AND THE EUROPEAN AMERICAN NEWSPAPER **NEW YORK**

Cable Address : Chicatrib-Paris
Telephones :
Trudaine 50-90. 50-91 & 50-92
Long distance (Inter-Trudaine 88)
» 115

Société Anonyme Française au Capital de Frs 100.000
R. C. Seine 107.256
5, RUE LAMARTINE, PARIS

Paris Information Office
1, Rue Scribe.
Telephone : Gutenberg 51-22
Theater Tickets : Gutenberg 09-31

August 20

My dear Mr. Loos :

I regret that you have had to make so many useless trips to the office in my absences.

Mr. Burke has left Paris and seems to have overlookedreturning your plans. I am writing him now requesting that he do so at once. He was greatly struck by them, particularly by you conception for the ground floor. But he had already retained his own American architects. There is still some doubt that he will actually build in Paris.

However, the Bowman Hotel interests seem to be intending to start work at an early date. Perhaps you could get in touch with them.

I shall mail you your plans as soon as they reach me.

There are two final pieces of evidence in this story. In the Loos Archive in the Albertina are a business card and a letter, both with the Paris address of the *Chicago Tribune*. They likely date from the year after the competition, 1923. The card, from a Mr. A. K. Small, has a handwritten address, 61, rue Lafayette, the headquarters of the *Petit Journal*, and a notation: "After 7 pm" (fig. 2.11). The letter, signed by a Jay P. Allen, informs Loos that a Mr. Burke (his identity is otherwise unknown; this does not seem to be the same Henry Burke who assisted Loos at the Salon d'Automne; perhaps it is his father?), for whom Loos made a house plan, had left Paris, and had "overlooked returning your plans" (fig. 2.12).[27] It adds that Mr. Burke was "greatly struck by them, particularly your conception for the ground floor," but notes that Burke had already retained an American architect.

It seems likely that the house for Mr. Burke—given the description of the lower floor—represents a lost *Raumplan* house. Do the card—presumably a reminder of a meeting—and the letter tell us something else? Did Loos continue to haunt the *Chicago Tribune* offices, in the vain hope that he might still convince someone there that his tower design should be built? Is that how he came to design a house for the mysterious Mr. Burke? I doubt we will ever know.

From the evidence we have, it seems that the drawings for the house were never returned to Loos. Even if he had been able to realize the Burke House, it would have been small recompense. His great Chicago tower remained unbuilt and tragically misunderstood.

|2.12. Letter from Jay P. Allen to Adolf Loos, August 20, [1923?], on *Chicago Tribune* letterhead. Adolf Loos Archiv, Albertina, Vienna, ALA 866v.

3 | Adolf Loos and the Lessons of the Vernacular

On the evening of December 8, 1910, Adolf Loos presented a lecture he titled "Über Architektur" at the Hagenhaus in Berlin. It was a short talk, perhaps less than an hour in duration, and unlike "Ornament and Crime," which Loos also presented a few times that year, far less controversial.

Loos gave the talk under the auspices of the Verein für Kunst, a local group of progressive artists and designers organized by the critic and art impresario Herwarth Walden. Loos subsequently published a small fragment of his speech in Walden's magazine, *Der Sturm* (fig. 3.1).[1] But the piece was not printed in its entirety until 1912, when it appeared, in French, in *Les Cahiers d'aujourd'hui.*[2] It was only much later, with the publication of Loos's book *Trotzdem*, in 1930, that it became widely available in German.[3]

Among Loos's essays, "Architektur," the essay's German title in its published form, is not as well known as "Ornament und Verbrechen" (Ornament and Crime), that singular eruption of Loos's convictions that remains the most often read, and the most commented upon, of his many texts. Still, those writing about Loos right up to the present quote frequently from "Architekur," in great part because it is one of Loos's few essays that bear directly on the problems of architectural design.

Ueber Architektur

Von Adolf Loos

Aus dem Vortrag, den Adolf Loos im Verein für Kunst hielt, sei hier eine kleine aber wichtige Stelle mitgeteilt.

Das Haus hat allen zu gefallen, zum Unterschiede vom Kunstwerk, das niemandem zu gefallen hat. Das Kunstwerk ist eine Privatangelegenheit des Künstlers. Das Haus ist es nicht. Das Kunstwerk wird in die Welt gesetzt, ohne dass ein Bedürfnis dafür vorhanden wäre. Das Haus deckt ein Bedürfnis. Das Kunstwerk ist niemandem verantwortlich, das Haus einem jedem. Das Kunstwerk will die Menschen aus ihrer Bequemlichkeit reissen, das Haus hat der Bequemlichkeit zu dienen. Das Kunstwerk ist revolutionär, das Haus ist konservativ. Das Kunstwerk weist der Menschheit neue Wege und denkt an die Zukunft, das Haus denkt an die Gegenwart. Wir lieben alles, was unserer Bequemlichkeit dient und uns bestätigt. Wir hassen alles, was uns aus unserer gesicherten Position reissen will und uns belästigt.

Und so lieben wir das Haus und hassen die Kunst. So also hätte das Haus nichts mit der Kunst zu tun und wäre die Architektur nicht unter die Künste einzureihen? Es ist so. Nur ein ganz kleiner Teil der Architektur gehört der Kunst an. Das Grabmal und das Denkmal. Alles andere, das einem Zweck dient, ist aus dem Reiche der Kunst auszuschalten.

|3.1. Adolf Loos, "Ueber Architektur." From *Der Sturm* (Berlin) 1, no. 42 (December 15, 1910): 334.

It is splendidly quotable. Loos gives us one of the most extraordinary images in the long history of musings about architecture and its meanings: "If we find a hill in a forest, six feet long and three feet wide, with a pyramidal mound atop it formed with a shovel, then we become solemn, and it speaks to us: here someone lies buried. *That is architecture.*"[4]

And, if that were not sufficient, Loos offers us perhaps the most perfect expression of the function of architecture as it relates to us as sensing human beings: "Architecture awakens feelings in people. The task of the architect, therefore, is to convey these feelings precisely. A room must be cozy (*gemütlich*), a house must appear liveable. A court of laws must appear threatening to those harboring secret vices. A bank must say: here your money is being kept safe and sound by honest people."[5]

What is mostly lost in the writings of later commentators is Loos's views on vernacular building and the lessons that it presents for modern architecture. This is an especially salient moment in his writings because it provides a clear insight into his distinctive way of approaching the design process.

Loos begins his essay with yet another extraordinary image:

> May I transport you to the banks of a mountain lake? The sky is blue, the water green, and everything rests in a deep peacefulness. The mountains and the clouds are reflected in the lake. So, too, are the houses, courtyards, and chapels! They stand there as if they had not been erected by the hand of man. They seem to have come from God's workshop, just as do the mountains and the trees, the clouds and blue sky. And everything breathes of beauty and quietude.[6]

Suddenly, this bucolic scene is interrupted: "There, what is that? Standing among the peasants' houses, but not from them . . . is a villa. The creation of a good or a bad architect? I do not know. I only know that peace, quiet, and beauty are lost.[7]

Loos's point, which he lays out relentlessly in the following pages, like a prosecuting attorney unfolding the case against the accused, is an assault on what he sees as the problems of architecture in his day: the striving of modern designers to express their individuality, their lack of a culture of their own, and their loss of faith in tradition. He recites, as he so often did in those years just before World War I, his objections to the improper use of ornament, even repeating his famed dictum from "Ornament and Crime" that the "*evolution of culture is synonymous with disappearance of ornament from objects of daily use*" (italics in the original).[8] He writes, too, about what he deems the overreliance on drawing by modern architects and how schools of architecture and design were fostering artificiality and "cultural barrenness."

Loos, as he also often did, offers an alternative. It is not quite a formula; rather, it is a lesson in a way of thinking. It is about how modern people, modern designers, might find a way out of their predicament. And here he is at his most potent as a thinker.

He begins with a simple question: Why is it that the house of the architect disturbs the mountain scene, but not that built by the peasant? (He contends that the creations of engineers, a railroad or ship, for instance, would fit equally well.)

The answer he gives is as direct and simple as his question: architects "make things differently." And it is in the concept of "making" that his true aim resides. Loos tells us that the peasant makes the place for his house in the earth; the mason uses the same local earth for bricks, or if the earth is not suitable, he employs local stone. In the same way, the carpenter makes the roof of local wood. "Is it beautiful or ugly?" Loos asks. His answer is wonderfully curt: "He doesn't know. It is a roof."[9] The same is true for the other tradesmen. They do their jobs; they follow their instincts and local tradition.

What Loos is telling us, of course, is that vernacular building practices are immediate and direct. They are shaped by what is available in terms of materials, and the forms arrived at through long experience. More to the point, though he does not use the word, they are not "contrived." Loos expresses this in a different way: "The craftsman cannot concern himself very much with books."[10]

What follows in the text is an attack on the artificiality of architecture in his time, on the overdependence on scholarship and elaborate graphic representation. Loos explains in detail how he believes this had all come about, how the search for a new style had led to a crisis of culture.

This part of the essay is very well known, and it is central to Loos's broader critique. He reveals one of his most luminous insights here: there is a fundamental difference between art and building. Most building is mundane, meant to serve us in ordinary ways. Only monumental building is art. The fact that these two spheres are so often conflated is the reason architects were failing to express the realities of the new age. Monumental architecture, Loos states unambiguously, is founded directly on the Western classical tradition. He insists that one need only continue and advance the ideas of Johann Bernhard Fischer von Erlach and Karl Friedrich Schinkel to produce good and appropriate monumental design.

Yet equally important is Loos's other major point, about how vernacular tradition could yet inform building. As usual, he draws distinctions to set up his argument. There is a fundamental difference, he submits, between building in the city and building in the country, just as there is a difference between an urban architecture of monumentality and ordinary building. If one comes to understand the reasoning behind vernacular traditions, then one can build well and genuinely in the country.

Loos, however, never quite lays out the specifics of how this might work—at least not in "Architektur." To get at this question, we must consider another of Loos's essays, "Regeln für den, der in den Bergen baut" (Rules for one building in the mountains). He published the piece in 1913 in the annual publication of the Schwarzwaldschule, a school founded and operated by his friend and patron Eugenie Schwarzwald.[11]

This text is direct in the way that "Architektur" is not: it presents a series of prescriptions and admonitions—a precise set of instructions—for any would-be architect seeking to understand the ways of vernacular building. It is rather short, extending in most printings only over a single page or two, and it is framed in seven brief paragraphs, the first sentence of each set out as a declarative statement:

> Do not build in a picturesque way.
> Build as well as you are able.
> Pay attention to the forms that the peasant builds with.
> A plain requires a vertical building form, the mountains a horizontal one.
> Think not about the roof; think about rain and snow.
> Take care! Nature can only abide the truth.
> Do not fear being criticized for not being modern.[12]

The messages are simple enough. So is the reasoning behind them, although it is at times more profound than one might imagine. Loos writes, for instance: "Think not about the roof; think about rain and snow." That seems obvious. But he appends a statement that is far more insightful:

> That is how the peasant thinks, and thus in the mountains he builds the flattest roof that his technical knowledge allows him. In the mountains, it is not a matter of enabling the snow to slide off when it will, but when the peasant wills it. The peasant must be able to climb onto the roof to remove the snow without endangering his life. We, too, have it as our responsibility to build the flattest roof we can with *our* technical means.[13]

That is unquestionably good sense, even if the point Loos is making is not fully evident at the outset. More importantly, it explains the inner reasoning of how one should draw from historical tradition and practice. Yet embedded in this rather banal bit of prose is an even more profound idea, one that extends to the core of Loos's thinking about architecture and modernity. Beyond the distinction he draws between "art" and "building" in "Architektur," Loos is addressing the fundamental problem of historicism and how to overcome it.

The historic revivalism of the second half of the nineteenth century was in part about ways to adapt older forms to new uses—the neo-Romanesque train station, for example, or slightly later, the neo-Gothic skyscraper. It was, in any event, a strategy for reapplying these past forms, which all too often were divorced from their original meanings. Historicism necessitated other alterations: in scale (as buildings increased in size), in syntax (as forms were arranged in new ways), and architectonically (as the forms often lost their structural rationales). What Loos is saying—obliquely but still with great resonance—is that it is not the forms themselves that matter, it is their underlying logic. Only when armed with this understanding could one build authentically and well. The role of the architect in modern times, thus, was to seek out those who still understood how the forms had come about and why. With this knowledge, the architect could determine whether any form could still be used, whether it might be "modern."

That one must seek out "those who know" is what lies behind Loos's description in "Architektur" of going "like a timid apprentice to the workshop and respectfully looking about for the man in the blue apron." He writes, "And I asked: let me be privy to your secrets." He then tells us what he discovered: that modernity in its purest form was already present everywhere in the crafts, "in the wooden panels of toilet tanks, the corner solution in silver chests."[14]

What Loos adds to this discussion is one of his defining notions: that architecture—and here once more he means "building"—is inherently an evolutionary enterprise. Any true change comes slowly because the rationale behind building undergoes only incremental adjustment. "I discovered," he tells us, "the most important thing, that the style of the year 1900 is only slightly different from that of 1800, in the way that the dress-coat of 1900 differs little from the dress-coat of 1800."[15]

It is a deep misunderstanding to think that Loos viewed radical change as normative. He was convinced that it is only when a true improvement is conceived that any dramatic alteration can (and should) come about. We can observe this readily in Loos's own design work. He "discovered" the *Raumplan*, his tactic of breaking up the standard arrangement of floors by making some rooms higher, others lower, all tightly arranged within the outer envelope of his buildings. (He

|3.2. Adolf Loos, Country House for Leo Prinz Sapieha (address unknown), 1918, variant version showing elevation of the side of the house. Adolf Loos Archiv, Albertina, Vienna, ALA 644.

claimed to have done so while sitting in a theater box and noticing that the view out to the larger space of the auditorium rendered the low ceiling of the box tolerable.) It conferred certain dividends, such as a saving of space. What was new and an improvement for Loos was permissible. Everything else, he was certain, should be derived from tradition, from practice, in an evolutionary fashion, until the models became outmoded or could no longer be improved upon.

These, then, were the guiding principles that Loos would apply when he came to build in the mountains. And equipped with this knowledge, one can read and interpret his designs.

Loos designed the first of his "mountain vernacular" houses in 1912 and 1913, a *Bauleitungshütte*, or temporary construction house, for the Schwarzwaldschule on Semmering mountain pass in Lower Austria.[16] A single drawing, which shows the plans, elevations, and a section, survives in the Loos Archive (Adolf Loos

3.3. Adolf Loos, Country House for Carla Spanner, Gumpoldskirchen, 1924. Adolf Loos Archiv, Albertina, Vienna, ALA 3232.

Archiv, Albertina, Vienna [hereafter ALA], 667). It is in the form of a heavy timber construction, with a pitched roof and full-height cross-dormers. Loos followed this project with several others, including one for Leo Prinz Sapieha in 1918 (intended location unknown; fig. 3.2) and another for a physician, a certain Dr. H., in Bad Gastein (ALA 2181) in 1922.[17] He also produced a modified country house with a flat roof for Carla Spanner in Gumpoldskirchen in 1924 (fig. 3.3).

It was not until 1928 that Loos would design the key work of his vernacular series, a country house for industrialist Paul Khuner.[19] He loosely based the scheme on the Sapieha House (figs. 3.4, 3.5). It is essentially a three-story structure with a large, open central hall on the main floor (fig. 3.6). Above, on the second level, is a mezzanine. The rooms are arranged around this space, connecting directly to it. In keeping with his beliefs, Loos adapted traditional forms for the exteriors of both houses. The executed Khuner House, however, features modern materials in many places, inside and out. More significantly, the house has a Raumplan built into it, with a complex entry sequence and rooms employing Loos's ideas of spatial diversity and economy (fig. 3.7).[19]

Some scholars have regarded the house as part of a longer history of Alpine building, which, of course, it is.[20] Yet it is not the borrowing of the forms themselves—Loos's appropriation of the Alpine vernacular—that is telling. Rather, it is that Loos believed that these forms were intrinsically part of a long tradition of building that was rooted in experience and knowledge of place, as well as climate, materiality, and usage. He did not see in the reapplication of the forms a direct and superficial borrowing, but rather a return to a deep-seated understanding. The forms, as such, were not the essential element; it was the wisdom in them—the result of long and continuous experimentation—that mattered. Loos, in that sense, had turned historicism on its head. He was interested not in a form of creative mimesis, but a full, ongoing dialogue with the past and its lessons.

The Khuner House also highlights the second aspect of Loos's belief in how to use the vernacular. Changes were permissible when they represented some genuine improvement. The use of modern materials—large sheets of glass, for example—was one such instance. More significant was his insertion of a Raumplan into a traditional mountain house form.

Yet even here, Loos made use of an older convention: the great hall of the English country manor house. Loos adapted a historical arrangement from an entirely different building culture and repurposed it. The entry sequence, which begins at the southeast (rear) corner, carries one up to the main living floor via a winding route through a *Windfang* (wind catchment), a vestibule, and a dou-

|3.4. Adolf Loos, Country House for Paul Khuner, Kreuzberg bei Payerbach, Austria, 1928–30. Photograph: Martin Gerlach, jun., ca. 1930. Albertina, Vienna, ALA 3165.

|3.5. Adolf Loos, Country House for Paul Khuner, Kreuzberg bei Payerbach, Austria, 1928–30. Photograph: Martin Gerlach, jun., ca. 1930. Albertina, Vienna, ALA 3176.

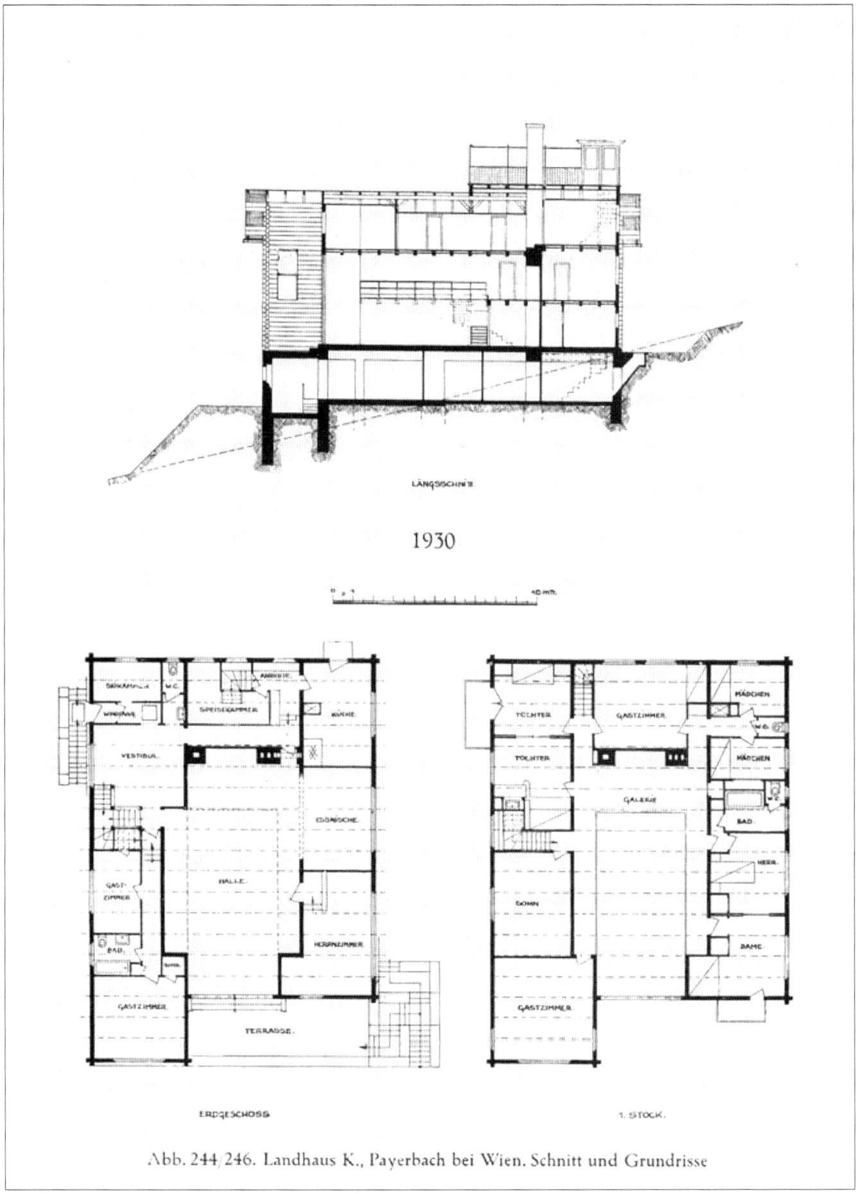

|3.6. Adolf Loos, Country House for Paul Khuner, Kreuzberg bei Payerbach, Austria, 1928–30. From Heinrich Kulka, *Adolf Loos: Das Werk des Architekten* (Vienna: Verlag Anton Schroll, 1931), figs. 244–46.

|3.7. Adolf Loos, Country House for Paul Khuner, Kreuzberg bei Payerbach, Austria, 1928–30, stair from the vestibule. Photograph: Wolfgang Thaler.

ble-sided stair. After completing this journey, one is left standing in the great hall. Above, arrayed on three sides (the fourth is mostly a great glass window wall), is the gallery, with another stair that continues to the uppermost level. The effect is that of the traditional English living hall (which often had balconies or galleries for musicians or other purposes) and, from above, Loos's concept of the theater box, with a lowered ceiling and vistas out into a larger volume.[21]

Loos was hardly alone in turning to the English hall as a domestic device. Many architects in Central Europe drew inspiration from Hermann Muthesius's *Das englische Haus*, published in three volumes from 1908 to 1911, which offered examples of such arrangements.[22] The strategy of exploiting the English hall form was entirely consistent with Loos's beliefs: it was time-tested and, on this occasion, an improvement, for it led to an enhancement of living spaces.

The Khuner House, then, is almost a diagram of Loos's intentions, of his strategies of appropriation. His adaptation of vernacular forms was a sign of his respect for tradition, of everything that had led up to them, what was rooted in each form. He saw no contradiction in the idea of appending modern enhancements to these vernacular forms. What is more, Loos's way of working within tradition, whether it involved "country" building or urban architecture, was intellectually consistent. Throughout his career, he advocated this reliance on disparate sources, as long as the underlying rules of operating—of designing—remained the same.

Loos's essay "Architektur" is thus a critique—of late historicism and what Loos saw as the deficiencies of the works of most of his fellow modernists. It is equally a call to action or, even better, a call for remediation. He describes the problem—the errant paths to the new design he was witnessing around him—and his solution, how to think properly about appropriation from the past and the generation of new forms. Despite its seeming emphasis on folk building, it is a complete and rigorous architectural program.

4 | Julius Posener on Adolf Loos

Several years ago, while doing research on Adolf Loos at the Canadian Centre for Architecture in Montréal, I chanced upon a thin yellow booklet. It contained a single essay on Loos written by Julius Posener.

I knew many of Posener's writings well, including the brilliant piece he had contributed to the exhibition catalogue Dietrich Worbs had put together on Loos's *Raumplan* concept in the 1980s.[1] This slight text, however, was new to me, and I read it with growing avidity, while sitting alone early one morning in the airy, high-ceilinged reading room.

I have always had a profound regard for Posener. He was the ultimate survivor, one of the last of his tribe. He was still writing, lecturing, and making frequent appearances on television and radio in the early 1990s, at a time when nearly all the other members of the modernist generation (to which he was a relative latecomer) had passed from the scene. Most had expired in the 1960s and 1970s, when I was too young to take in what they had accomplished. But Posener was very much alive as I first came to understand and appreciate all they had wrought.

In person, Posener had an affecting presence. Even when he was not speaking, he possessed a quiet, knowing dignity. And his pronouncements for me always had a certain ringing clarity. He was an authentic voice about modernism's early history.

Born in Berlin in 1904 to a well-to-do and cultivated Jewish family, Posener had come of age when the modern movement in architecture was just beginning to coalesce. He seems to have come to his late role instinctively. He was deeply cultured in the way that few people are today. His father, Moritz Posener, was a landscape and portrait painter who once exhibited with the Berlin Secessionists; his musical mother came from one of Berlin's great real estate families. The couple built an English-style villa in the leafy environs of Lichterfelde-West as a statement of their progressivism in architecture and in life.

After finishing his studies at the Berlin Technische Hochschule, Posener embarked on an extended sojourn, carried along on the wave of ascendant modernism. Yet, much like Loos, he neither started nor ended as a conventional modernist. He was, instead, as his son Alan Posener observed in an email to me, a modernist "by default."[2]

Julius Posener's imperfect conversion to modernism had begun almost as soon as he commenced his studies. This happened, as Alan Posener explained, not because he was a convinced modernist at the time, but "because the conservatives to whom he was most attracted—the architect Erich Blunck for instance, in whose course he enrolled as a freshman at the Technische Hochschule, or Heinrich Tessenow, whom he always admired—had, by the 1920s, become reactionaries, or at least figureheads for the reactionaries. Julius was the only Jew in Blunck's class, and the other students made him feel it. After a short time, he fled to Hans Poelzig, who was not a modernist in the same way that Erich Mendelsohn was."[3]

Posener became a protégé (and later biographer) of Poelzig. Most of all, though, Posener wanted to assimilate, to become, in the words of his son, a "mildly progressive German bourgeois." In this, he was simply following the lead of his parents, who had moved to Lichterfelde precisely because it was not one of the heavily "Jewish" suburbs "like Grunewald or Zehlendorf." But Julius's experiences at the Technical University soon disabused him of the idea. The subtle and overt antisemitism of many of the students and teachers meant that Julius found himself associating primarily with the other Jewish students at the school. Seeking their own, separate path, they formed the modernist Arbeitskreis der neuen Form (Working Group of the New Form). The group emerged, as Alan Posener observed, "more out of opposition to the rising tide of antisemitism, which went hand in hand with anti-modernism, than to—on Julius's part—any real admiration for the work of, say, Mendelssohn."[4]

This was part of the splendid irony that marked much of his later career: "That Julius ended up working for Mendelsohn in Jerusalem had much more to do with, to put it bluntly, Hitler, than with any decision on his part that was pro-modernist." Later, Posener built his only house in Kfar Shmaryahu near Tel Aviv. It was, in the words of his son, "definitely not modernist." Mendelsohn's comment was "Mein armer Junge! [My poor boy!]."[5]

But Posener's relationship to modernism was always drifting. Long before he set foot in Palestine, Posener had become the first paid employee of *L'Architecture d'aujourd'hui*, the leading French journal on the new architecture, when it began publication in 1930. In the early 1930s, he returned briefly to Berlin, but soon after Hitler came to power in 1933, he left (propelled by a firm nudge from his mother) on what would become a twenty-eight-year exile, living and working in Jerusalem, London, and Kuala Lumpur. He finally went back to the city of his youth in 1961, to begin one of modernism's greatest second acts, as a teacher, critic, historian, and sage.

Posener was ten when World War I broke out; he was, accordingly, much too young to have witnessed Loos's early battles. Later, when he began to study architecture in Berlin, in those first heady years of the Weimar Republic, Loos was mostly absent from the international scene. If Posener observed much about Loos at that time, it would have been from afar. He discovered Le Corbusier in 1929, during his first stay in Paris. His verdict then, after taking in the shoddiness of construction that afflicted Corbusier's early Paris villas, was brutally rendered: "Anyone who builds that badly is no architect." Posener changed his mind a few years later, after a visit to the newly finished Villa Savoye. "This was an architecture I could not even have imagined," he wrote.[6]

Posener, though, could never quite make his peace with the mainstream of the later modern movement. All his life, he had a strong affinity for the mitigated modernism of the pre–World War I era and for a select set of buildings from the 1920s. Alan Posener's assessment of his father's career paints a wholly different picture from other commentators, who generally regarded Posener as a tried-and-true modernist.[7]

> Back in Berlin, Julius became famous—or notorious—for his attempts to save villas by Hermann Muthesius, his hero, which in the 1960s and 1970s were being torn down to make way for apartment blocks. This was an anti-modernist stance, and he never accepted the ideology of the "autogerechte Stadt" [the car-centric city] based on Corbusier's ideas or the Athens Charter. So, I think he saw in Loos a kindred spirit, a man

> who rejected historicism and "ein Leben im Falschen" [a life of falsehood] but was never happy with the brashness of modernism—or with modernity, for that matter. In his writings, Julius underscores Muthesius's modernness and Corbusier's "architecturalness," but the most important thing for him was . . . "decorum." I think it is precisely this hesitancy to throw in his lot with the Modernists, this feeling that somehow architecture—and European culture—had in many ways peaked before the catastrophe of 1914, that made him interesting in West-Berlin, which in the sixties was busy exorcising the past and throwing out whole hordes of kids with the bathwater. Later, in the 1980s and 1990s, when postmodernism reared its ugly head, claiming him as one of its prophets, he insisted, as I say, on the architectural value of what Mendelsohn, Bruno and Max Taut, Le Corbusier, and the others had done: Not the Unitè d'Habitation, which he hated, but the Villa Savoye or the houses in the Weißenhofsiedlung. Not the Einstein Tower, which he considered a fake, but the Weizmann villa in Rehovot. And so on.[8]

Posener's vision of Loos was undoubtedly colored by his own experiences and views. Still, for the next three decades after he left Paris, Posener was far from Vienna and even farther from Adolf Loos's special orbit. How was it then, I asked myself as I read further into the little yellow booklet (a published version of the address Posener presented at the opening of Dietrich Worbs's 1983 exhibition of Loos's domestic Raumplan ideas), that his insight and verdicts were so spot on? (Posener's essay appears in English translation in the appendix.) Why in those few pages was Posener able to present such a limpid and discerning portrait of Loos, his ideas, and his context?

It took me a while to work it out. Part of the answer is that Posener must have kept reading and reflecting on modernism during all those years of his own personal hegira. Late in his life, in Berlin, he was a professor for more than a decade at the Hochschule für Bildende Künste. He wrote extensively on the history of architecture, especially on the early history of modernism. I am quite sure he came to know the standard literature on Loos in this period. It was at that time, from the mid- to late 1960s through the early 1970s, that Loos was being rediscovered.

What Posener understood, and too many observers and critics had overlooked, was that a significant part of Loos's intellectual formation took place not in the era of budding modernism but in the period just before, in the early 1890s, when historicism was still vital, and its discontents were not yet fully visible. In that way, Loos belonged in company with some of the other modernists who came of age at that time. The late Philip Johnson wickedly remarked—more than once, and in what was certainly one of the best put-downs in the history of architecture—that Frank Lloyd Wright was "the greatest architect of the nineteenth century."[9] The corollary, following Posener's line of thought, might be that Adolf Loos was the greatest architectural writer and thinker of the late nineteenth century. Both statements are mordantly amusing in themselves, but there is more to them than that. Johnson was at least partially correct: Wright recast the Victorian house, church, and office building into something else; his efforts, though, were more often transformative (in the strict sense of the word) than entirely revolutionary. Only later in his life—really, from the period of around 1914 on—was Wright engaged in a more radical set of pursuits. The many houses and other works of Wright's Oak Park years and just after were still mostly part of an older discourse about building and living.

It is not quite correct to say that Loos's intellectual horizons did not extend beyond the 1890s. He certainly showed an awareness of the controversies that followed. But he stood apart from those times. Loos's own attacks on modern ornament and a contrived architecture *sound* modern, and they have always been read that way. Loos's early villas (and even his odd-duckling Haus am Michaelerplatz) *look* more or less modern, but they are ultimately more about a repudiation of what had come before than a pure portent of what modernism would be. Posener understood this. Loos, he writes,

> belonged neither to the epoch in which his design came to fruition nor to the earlier one. He remained apart from the ideals of the avant-garde of the years before 1914 just as much as he held his distance from the ideals of the avant-garde before 1933. And certainly, he stayed away from the reactionaries of both epochs. If he felt—with a despair bordering on complacency—that he was a stranger in his time, a being sui generis, a man of a time yet to come, he was right: he was a being sui generis, a man of a time yet to come.[10]

Posener detected something else in Loos's writings and buildings. Other, later commentators have noted it as well, without quite being able to articulate it with the same coruscating precision: in crucial ways, Loos was not a radical; on the contrary, he was remarkably conservative. Posener identified two areas in which this essential quality is manifest:

> The problem that brought the Werkbund into being, namely the deterioration in the quality of products caused by the introduction of the machine, does not seem to have attracted Loos's attention, although he must have encountered the phenomenon, if not in Austria, then certainly in America. What is unexpected is the conservative standpoint we can detect in his writings.
>
> Speaking of his conservative attitude, allow me to mention another development (the first was the rise of industrial production) that greatly concerned his contemporaries, but which apparently was of no interest to Loos: construction. The two central themes of the years around the turn of the century were really the problem of serial production on the one hand and, on the other, the relationship of architecture to new materials and construction methods. Loos was not truly touched by this development, either; reading his work, one comes away with the impression that architectural construction had not advanced beyond that which had served Michelangelo, or, to put it less pretentiously, the simple builders of simple houses. Loos does mention Otto Wagner, the newest star in the architectural firmament. But about the bold glass roof construction in Wagner's Postal Savings Bank, Loos has nothing to say.[11]

Here, Posener misses the mark. It is true that Loos had little interest in the problem of industrial production. He seems to have held firm to his assumption that the most important objects of daily use (*Gebrauchsgegenstände*)—from furniture to clothing—would continue to be handmade by consummate craftspeople. He never really considers, as Josef Hoffmann did in his Wiener Werkstätte manifesto, the impact of industrial production on such wares.[12] In the Vienna of Loos's time, it was still possible—precisely because the traditional crafts remained alive for much longer than in Germany—to live in a manner that was mostly unaffected by industrialization. What is unsaid in Loos's writings is that this reality was closely tied to class. The Viennese bourgeoisie (and their counterparts in interwar Czechoslovakia, where Loos also had many clients) could afford to live in a fashion that mostly ignored the realities of the machine. They could still pay for a pair of handcrafted shoes; the working class in either country not so much. Many of Loos's clients earned their money as modern factory owners but lived domestically as their parents had, in a world where everything was still custom-fitted and precisely made to the client's wishes.

Posener sees this far more plainly than most observers. Where he is not quite right is in his assessment of Loos's attitudes toward construction. Loos did not entirely ignore the possibilities of modern materials and building methods; they were just not very important for him. He had a firm grasp on the newest construction techniques: he had first attended the architecture course at the Staatsgewerbeschule (State Trades School) in Brünn (now Brno), and he subsequently spent two years at the Technical University in Dresden. He could hardly have missed the many lessons about new ways to build. And when Loos needed to employ new building methods, as he did in the multi-storied Goldman & Salatsch building, he showed no hesitancy at all. (Underneath its conservative cladding, the building is a cutting-edge, reinforced concrete-frame structure, executed by what was then one of the most advanced building firms in Central Europe, Pittel & Brausewetter.) And later, when it was required, he experimented with modern wood construction (based on American models), or he used poured-concrete floors, columns, and stairs.[13] But Loos, unlike Wagner (and here Posener is undoubtedly correct), did not believe that new construction methods per se should be the driving force of the new architecture. Loos thought of construction as a "tool," not as an imperative. In that, he was out of step with not only many of the younger modernists in Vienna, but also most of those across Europe and in the United States.

The reasons for this Posener understood fully. One he only alludes to; the other he discusses at some length.

What Posener knew all too well is that Loos's approach to architecture was essentially cultural. Loos believed that any architectural construct should reflect the culture that made it and, conversely, that one's culture should be the driving force behind any set of architectural choices. Many, if not most, of Loos's writings are focused, with nearly laser-like precision, on those places where he detects a disconnect between a given culture (almost always "his"!) and design decisions that violated the key constituents of that culture. This is the basis of Loos's critique of Hoffmann and the other Secessionists: they were making a "contrived" design that was out of step with modern Viennese reality. The whole of his essay "Ornament and Crime" is predicated on this notion.

Posener, as I said, understood this. What he found even more arresting in Loos's thinking, though, was his fundamental conservativism. Loos was never a conservative in the mode of the historicists—of those seeking to hold on to the past at all costs, even if that meant making a mash-up of it. Loos sees the manipulations of historical form-languages that had been commonplace in his youth not as an act of reverence, but as a savage abuse of history. His conservatism was of a wholly different stripe. Loos esteemed not the forms of the historical past per se but the broader ideal of continuity. He believed that Europeans, especially those who lived in regions that had once been part of the Roman dominion (like Vienna), were inextricably bound up with Greco-Roman tradition. This truth for him was unassailable.

He drew two lessons from his conviction. The first was that the forms of classicism still had legitimacy. The second was that the logic of classical building did as well and that it should be a guide to building in the present. That did not mean for Loos that one should slavishly follow the classical rulebook, but rather that the underlying principles retained their power and meaning. Order, symmetry, discipline, decorum (in the Vitruvian sense), and restraint were all still valid and necessary.

Posener, who perceives this perfectly, writes: "Again and again, [Loos] states that the great architects all looked back to antiquity, that architecture, despite the periodic fluctuations of the zeitgeist, would remain the most conservative art. He names these greats: Schlüter, Fischer von Erlach, Schinkel, 'the great tamer of the imagination,' and Semper."[14]

The key phrase Posner uses here is "the great tamer of the imagination" (*der große Bändiger der Phantasie*). It is worth taking a moment to unpack its meaning because it is key to so much that Loos held dear. The German word *Phantasie* (in the spelling from that time) is slightly different in meaning from "imagination," which in English does not necessarily imply the same free unfolding of a designer's will. But Loos's understanding of *Phantasie* is closely tied to a sense of undisciplined creativity. It is exactly the sort of contrived, "made-up" aesthetic that Loos accused the Secessionists of forging, a modernism that was made willy-nilly. The recourse to the classical tradition for Loos was a means to impose limits, to ensure that designers worked within certain "established" boundaries.

It was also a means of reining in excess. Posener writes: "[J]ust as the discipline of classical antiquity had served to counter the excesses of the Baroque, it could now also serve as a corrective to the excesses of the Secession." In design terms, Loos's own response to the wayward aesthetic of the Secession was to emphasize conventional principles, such as axiality and symmetry.

Posener detects that Loos became more conservative in this regard over time. In his early years, he often borrowed and adapted the English Arts and Crafts aesthetic, which allowed for a "freer" design style. From the time of the war on, however, Loos became more "classical," more fully wedded to strict ordering. This is most apparent when he is composing in two dimensions (the elevations of façades, walls, and certain interior or exterior vignettes). His spatial configurations, however, are guided by a different set of assumptions. They hew closely to Loos's ideas about the patterns of living—more precisely, to the patterns of bourgeois living.

It is in this regard that Posener taught me something I had never grasped completely: namely, that the Raumplan, in addition to its space-saving and "experiential" functions, was Loos's way of avoiding traditional spatial arrangements while still imposing order.

Posener spells this out with wonderful precision:

> The Raumplan replaces the classical-hierarchical principle with one that one could paraphrase with the word "convenience," which, however, does not mean a *functional* convenience: on the contrary. . . . I'm thinking more of something like serenity: a free and generous relationship of the volumes to each other. The symmetries serve only to indicate that one should behave here, regardless of the looseness of the planning. The elegant and emphatically displayed materials—marble, fine woods—also serve to underscore this. Apparently, this admixture of freedom and form was very important to Loos.[15]

It is Posener's last statement on this theme, though, that makes it so persuasive: "[I]f one examines the Raumplan—and the symmetries and the beautiful materials—but especially the Raumplan, and once again the Raumplan, you can get a—faint—idea of the considered constraint that prevailed in such rooms."[16]

The Raumplan, in other words, serves also to impose a social order—or better, a "ritual" order. Loos's intention was to shape specific patterns of behavior in accord with the expectations of a Central European bourgeoisie: how one "should" enter a house, receive guests, have an intimate dinner with friends, or retire to a private domain. And equally important here: how the servants should live and work within the larger frame of the house. The Raumplan is both a guide and a "restraining" feature. It is a replacement for the ordering of the old bourgeois *Palais,* without jettisoning its specific patterns of living.

Posener knew all this because it is the world in which he grew up. Even with the alterations of Loos's Raumplan, he recognized the patterns, the rituals, as those of his youth. His eyes, still adjusted to a culture and a time that had long ceased to exist, saw all this effortlessly.

5 | Adolf Loos and His Contemporaries

The recently published edition of Otto Wagner's late diary, covering the years from 1915 to 1918, offers piercing insights into his personality, his activities, and his sorrows in the period just prior to his death.[1] Through Wagner's eyes, we glimpse the fading world of Habsburg Vienna in its last, fitful throes. The cafés and salons in Wagner's account still hum with the voices of the *culturati* and *literati*, but skulking just beneath the surface is a sense of impending disaster.

Wagner notes the decline he sees everywhere around him. In his entry for February 12, 1917, for instance, he begins "Heißgeliebte!" ("Dearly beloved one!"—for all his entries are addressed to his wife, Louise, who had died in 1915): "No movies, no streetcars, the war is awful, everything is death. And then there is the terrible cold; I have frostbite on my heels."[2]

Reading the roughly 230 pages of entries (splendidly edited and annotated by Andreas Nierhaus and Alfred Pfoser) is equally depressing and instructive. Still discernable are the traces of the *Wiener Moderne* as it had been before the war, and most of its dramatis personae appear in Wagner's entries. We encounter Josef Hoffmann, Leopold Bauer (Wagner's successor at the Akademie der bildenden Künste), Gustav Klimt, Koloman Moser, Arthur Schnitzler, and many others. Even some of the lesser Viennese modernist architects appear in these pages, including Robert Oerley (or Örley), Hans Prutscher, and Otto Schönthal. But palpable throughout is Wagner's increasing bitterness. He is often irascible, petty, and mean-spirited. He is clearly a human being on the decline, making a not very graceful exit.

For scholars of Adolf Loos, there is a glaring gap in Wagner's late diary. The book's index includes the names of more than two hundred people, everyone from Peter Behrens to Otto von Bismarck. Yet Wagner does not mention Adolf Loos a single time. There is anti-Semitism, snobbery, backbiting, and resentment, but there is nothing at all about Loos, not even a casual aside.

The truth is that Loos mattered little to Wagner. And what was true for Wagner was also true for many—even most—of his contemporaries. It was especially true for those like Wagner, who were older than Loos and belonged to very different architectural lineages. For most of the two decades before the outbreak of World War I, Loos was barely a subject for the old guard—those who had begun their practices during the ascendancy of historicism. He was never a part of their world. Nor was he a part of any of the standard groupings of fin-de-siècle architects and designers. He was not a Secessionist or a Hagenbündler. And during World War I, Loos was not even the consummate outsider. For many, like Wagner, he was beneath notice.

Later, after the war, Loos remained outside the mainstream of the modern movement. He was not a modernist in the usual sense because he never subscribed to the idea that a new architecture required the rejection of all that had come before. And when other architects did pay attention to him, it was because he provoked unease in them, or even alarm. Carl König once posted a notice on the bulletin board of his studio at the Vienna Technische Hochschule forbidding students from attending Loos's impromptu architecture lectures at the nearby Café Museum, so troubled was he about the pernicious effect Loos was having on them.[3]

From the start, the Viennese critics issued a mixed verdict on Loos and his work. Ludwig Hevesi, the city's leading turn-of-the-century modernist critic, offered an insightful, if not entirely flattering, review of Loos's Café Museum (figs. 5.1, 5.2). "Loos presents himself as an outspoken anti-Secessionist in his Café Museum." It is "well done. Somewhat nihilistic, very nihilistic, but appetizing, logical, and practical. . . . And unexpected, which is also an achievement. You have no idea how difficult it is to make something unexpected and yet have it be enlightening."[4]

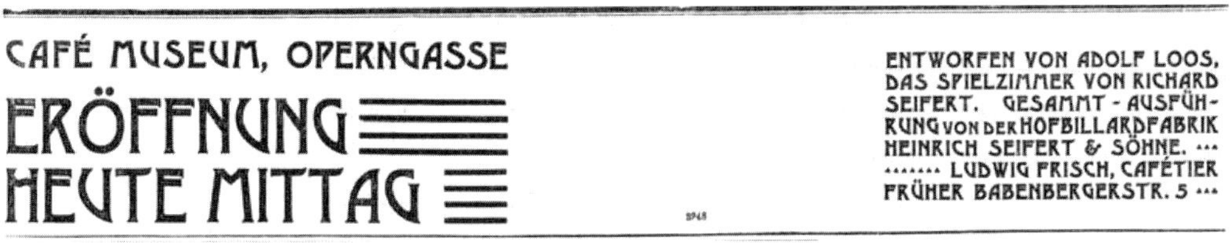

|5.1. Advertisement announcing the opening of the Café Museum in the *Arbeiter Zeitung*, April 19, 1899.

|5.2. Adolf Loos, Café Museum, Vienna, 1899. Adolf Loos Archiv, Albertina, Vienna, ALA 2495.

Mostly, though, Hevesi did what the other Viennese critics did: they ignored Loos. Or they dismissed him, often with patronizing asides. Hevesi refers to one particularly spartan bedroom ensemble (by the cabinetmaker firm of Friedrich Otto Schmidt) exhibited at the 1901 Winter exhibition at the Österreichisches Museum für angewandte Kunst simply as "à la Loos."[5] Later, in 1907, in his review of Loos's Steiner Decorative Feather Store on the Kärntnerstraße, he had fun at Loos's expense: "People stand in front of the shop and stare. Whose work is that? Loos. Oh, yes, Loos! It certainly looks like him."[6] And on yet another occasion, referring to Loos's 1908 competition design for the new War Ministry building, he describes it as "intentionally inconspicuous," as if to render it thereby somehow inconsequential. (To be fair, Hevesi does praise the design's "affective" main façade.)[7]

Only once, in those years before the war, did the critics pay particular attention to Loos: during the controversy over his so-called Haus am Michaelerplatz. Most of the responses to Loos's design can only be described as "withering." Hugo Wittmann, writing in the *Neue Freie Presse*, the city's leading liberal newspaper, described Loos's building as a "stab in the heart" of Vienna, and a "sad scantiness."[8] Others branded the building as the "grain elevator" (*Getreidespeicher*), the "dung crate" (*Mistkiste*), the "prison" (*Gefangenhaus*), the "crude crate" (*gehobelte Kiste*), the "dresser-drawer building" (*Schubladenkastenbau*), or the "house without eyebrows" (*Haus ohne Augenbrauen*).[9] Karl Rykl, a member of the city council, called it "a monstrosity" (*ein Scheusal*).[10]

And most of Loos's critics were no kinder to him personally. Hans Schneider, another member of the city council, referred to his design as "amateurish." Others muttered behind his back that he might be a little—or more than a little—unhinged. Loos, who had "built an American building," one observer wrote, "was mocked and made the butt of jokes."[11] And, at the height of the controversy, people hurled insults at Loos on the street.[12] Karl Marilaun, writing a decade afterward, described the continued response from the public: "Loos was the man, who—yes, indeed—despoiled the Michaelerplatz. A fool [*Narr*]. A weirdo [*Sonderling*]. An unpleasant man [*unbequemer Mensch*]."[13]

All of which might make one suppose that Loos occupied a more central position in the early history of modernism than he did. Loos had his moments. He drew much attention in 1898, with the publication in the *Neue Freie Presse* of his series of brilliant (and often irascible) commentaries on the Jubilee Exhibition, held in the Prater that late spring, summer, and fall. His readers at the time found Loos's weekly feuilletons annoying and amusing—seemingly in about the same measure. Few appear to have drawn much from his often-brilliant insights, however, because they were so far out of the mainstream of architectural and aesthetic thinking at the time. Loos again attracted attention in 1907, when he gave public tours of some of the apartments he had designed.[14] And his Kärntnerbar, in Vienna, which opened the following year, was a topic of discussion for many Viennese—at least briefly.

Loos's international fame came only when he began lecturing publicly. His first talk (a dry run of sorts for what would become "Ornament and Crime") took place in Berlin in December 1909, which he followed with public talks in Vienna,

Berlin, Munich, Prague, and elsewhere.[15] These events included versions of "Ornament and Crime," "Architecture," and some of his other of his well-known essays of the period—often in combination.[16] In 1908, Loos also published several articles in the Munich-based magazine *März* (whose editors included the noted writers Hermann Hesse and Ludwig Thoma), which cast him a little more into the spotlight—a little more.[17]

Mostly, though, until the period immediately after the war, Loos remained a local personality, a particularly Viennese phenomenon. And even then, he was more a periodic "topic of discussion" than a continual presence.

He was certainly a man about town. He was always elegantly dressed, the writer Emil Szittya remembered, and many "older women were in love with him."[18] He had a small following among the young *revoltés*. But he was otherwise not much respected, especially within the ranks of the city's foremost architects. He had his friends, but his professional attachments were few. He befriended the architect Robert Oerley, himself something of an outsider, who, early on, had praised Loos's Café Museum. But none of Loos's commissions originated from within the Viennese professional architectural orbit; throughout his career, he relied almost exclusively on the work that came to him from his friends, their relatives, and a limited coterie of admirers. He never won an architectural competition—in great measure because he stopped submitting to them, but just as much because no one inside the profession was willing to champion him when it mattered. Even at the height of the Michaelerplatz controversy, Loos found almost no vocal supporters among the ranks of Vienna's leading architects.

Outside Vienna, especially across Central Europe, people with some interest in art and culture watched and took in Loos's struggles. He found some sympathy, more among writers and journalists than architects, and gradually his message about ornament—in essence, that it no longer had a place or a raison d'être in modern life—began to be heard. Progress was slow, however, because for the decade after 1910 Loos published almost nothing. Those who had heard his public talks circulated his ideas—frequently in bastardized form. But they had few texts to refer to. One exception was "Ornament and Crime," which appeared in a French translation in 1912.[19] (The essay was not published in German until the end of the 1920s.[20])

Loos's appearance as an architect with a broader European reach came only in the 1920s. From 1921 to 1924, he headed the Vienna municipal *Siedlungsamt*, which was charged with overseeing the construction of various low-density public and private housing developments in and around the city. Loos's efforts drew attention from observers across Europe, curious to see what he and Vienna's new Socialist municipal government could achieve.

More crucial was Loos's growing attachment to Paris. In the early summer of 1920, shortly after making a visit to Paris with his new wife, Elsie Altmann-Loos, Loos received an invitation to exhibit his work at the forthcoming Salon d'Automne. He had received a similar invitation in 1914, but the outbreak of the war had precluded his participation. The new invitation strengthened Loos's resolve to take up permanent residence in the city. He and Elsie traveled there again in September 1920, and Loos, aided by Elsie and a young American named Henry Burke, spent three days preparing the exhibit, which included drawings, photographs, and a large model of Loos's 1913 project for a hotel on the Semmering mountain pass. Among those who saw the display were Le Corbusier and the Japanese painter Tsugouharu Foujita.[21]

Afterward, Loos decided to stay in Paris through October. He entered into discussions about publishing his early essays with the house of George Crès et Cie.[23] During mid-October, while Loos and Elsie were still in residence, Le Corbusier republished "Ornament and Crime" in French, in his magazine *L'Esprit nouveau*.[23]

Loos was now more resolved than ever to move to Paris. He finally did so in the summer of 1924, after resigning his post at the Siedlungsamt. (He reportedly turned down an offer from Chaim Weizmann, one of the leaders of the Zionist movement, to go to Palestine and help build the new Jewish state.[24])

Loos spent a good part of the next four years in the French capital. But as young French scholar Cécile Poulot shows in her recent excellent dissertation on this period of Loos's life and work, he was forced to travel back to Central Europe repeatedly to find commissions and supervise work already under construction. The reason for this was that Loos found it very difficult to secure commissions in Paris. He spoke little French, his deafness was becoming progressively worse, and he lacked the money and the requisite connections in Paris to develop a thriving practice. He did have an active social life there: Loos was always adept at meeting artists, writers, and other cultural figures (fig. 5.3). Nevertheless, he was never firmly rooted in the Parisian modern architectural circles. Over time, Le Corbusier and others began to view him with some disdain. In consequence, Loos's personal acquaintances were mostly outsiders and recent immigrants. Eventually, he gathered a small group of architects around him, foreigners in the main, including some who had attended Loos's private *Bauschule* in Vienna.[25]

|5.3. Loos, third from the right, with others outside the Café du Dôme, Paris, August 1926. Among those present were Loos's former student, Zlatko Neumann from Zagreb (fourth from the right in conversation with Loos), and Dutch painter Piet Mondrian (second from the right). Apart from the sculptor Michel Seuphor (on the far right), almost everyone else in the photograph was originally from Central Europe. Collection of Martin Gerlach, Vienna.

|5.4. Celebration in honor of Adolf Loos's sixtieth birthday on December 10, 1930. Loos is seated at the center; Josef Gočár is seated second from the left. Author's collection.

That Loos was essentially isolated in Paris is not in itself surprising. The Paris of the interwar years was awash with "colonies" of foreigners, most of whom remained on the periphery of Parisian cultural life. There was, for example, the large American expat group of artists, writers, and hangers-on, which had its own independent dynamic; and there were similar collectives of Germans, Russians, other Eastern Europeans "coexisting" in Paris, though not necessarily overlapping with the French modernist architectural or artistic circles. Even in Le Corbusier's atelier, the many foreigners who worked for him (including a rather sizeable group of Czechs) formed their own, discrete world.[26]

This period was important for Loos in terms of expanding the reach of his ideas and works (especially, but not exclusively, in France and Czechoslovakia). Yet it also reveals again how far outside *any* mainstream Loos was. Though he was often in Czechoslovakia in this period and afterward, overseeing the work on various projects and conferring with clients, he formed few connections within the large Czech modernist architectural community. One conspicuous bit of evidence for this is the fact that of the leading Czech architects, only Josef Gočár attended the dinner celebrating Loos's sixtieth birthday celebration in Prague (fig. 5.4).[27]

It was around the time of Loos's sixtieth birthday, at the end of 1930, that the second volume of his writings, *Trotzdem 1900–1930,* appeared.[28] The book collected most of Loos's later writings—those he had written and/or published in the wake of the Jubilee pieces, which made up the core of *Ins Leere gesprochen*. (The latter was also republished in 1932.) For the first time, Loos's most important later essays, including "Ornament and Crime," "Architecture," and "The Superfluous Ones," became readily available. Up to this juncture, anyone who wanted to read Loos had to find his articles in a motley set of newspapers and magazines, published in several different countries—something few people would have taken the trouble to do. They simply read this or that article, as they came across them.

It is not just that Loos was not much read up to the early 1930s (and beyond; he was "rediscovered" only in the 1960s). His design work was not much seen, either. In his superb and enlightening doctoral thesis "Who Has Seen Adolf Loos? Images of Adolf Loos's Architecture in the Media, 1899–1927," recently completed at the Akademie der bildenden Künste in Vienna, Max Moya took on the question of the representation of Adolf Loos's buildings and plans in publications during Loos's lifetime.[29]

Am Michaelerplatz.

Landmann: Ah, das neuche Gefangenhaus!
Kikeriki: Aber, aber, das ist das modernste Modehaus!

|5.5. "Am Michaelerplatz." From *Kikeriki*, February 5, 1911, 3. The inscription reads, "Farmer: Oh, the new prison! *Kikeriki* reporter: Oh, no, on the contrary, that is the building in the most modern fashion!" Österreichische Nationalbibliothek, Vienna.

Despite a diligent search, Moya found a mere 120 images related to Loos in the twenty-eight years covered by his study—the years of Loos's career before he returned to Vienna in 1928. These include not only interiors and individual pieces of furniture, but also a few cartoons (fig. 5.5).

Moya found that a small number of photographs, fifty-five in all, appeared before 1923, a paltry sum if one compares Loos's publication record with Otto Wagner's at the height of his career. As Moya writes, Loos's time in Paris would dramatically increase the number of Loosian images in the media, "but not precisely because of the French capital itself. Rather it seems that the pivotal event was Loos's participation in the 1923 Paris Salon d'Automne exhibition. If Loos made his first significant literary debut in France in 1912, his significant *visual* debut in France took place in 1923."[30]

Many of the leading French modernist architecture and design publications cast a light on Loos. In the roughly four years Loos was "based" in Paris, in part because of the greater publicity he received in France, some Austrian, Dutch, German, and Czechoslovak journals also began to show increased attention to his architecture. Loos's "celebrity," such as it was, grew accordingly. He even made it into Paris *Vogue* a few times in 1927. The quintessential fashion magazine published several of his projects, including his little-known stables for Prince Sangusko in Poland.[31]

Still, the most important avant-garde publications of the 1920s—*G: Material zur elementaren Gestaltung*, *Veshch/Gegenstand/Object*, or *Die Form*, for example—ignored Loos entirely. And what was true of the progressive architectural press was also true of the important modernist exhibitions of the 1920s. One of the most telling indications of Loos's lowly reputation among the modernists is that he was left off the final list of architects invited to design and build a house at the 1927 Stuttgart Weißenhofsiedlung. Loos was briefly considered, but in the end the organizers of the exhibition, most notably Ludwig Mies van der Rohe, who oversaw the project, rejected him. And not only for the housing portion of the exhibition: he was also not invited to show his work at the accompanying exhibit of new furniture and interiors.[32]

Some of the leading modernists in Germany viewed Loos as a contrarian; others—more damagingly—regarded him as a has-been. This was due in the main to the generally low regard with which the Germans saw the works of the Viennese in this period. (Josef Frank was the only Viennese modernist given the honor of building a house at Stuttgart, and even Frank's "comfortable" aesthetic was suspect for some.) It also issued from a sense that Loos himself—and his architecture and views—were not in accord with the mainstream of the modern movement. The most pointed confirmation of this came the next year, when Loos was not invited to attend the first meeting of the Congrès Internationaux d'Architecture Moderne (CIAM) in La Sarraz.

So Loos spent his last years mostly as an outsider, occasionally fulminating about his exclusion.[33] That he would build what was his true masterpiece, the Villa Müller in Prague, in this period, and that he would greatly expand and refine his *Raumplan* concept, went almost entirely unheeded, except in Prague, where in the last years of his life he achieved a sort of celebrity status. The daily newspapers there followed his movements closely and reported on his activities.

Loos, of course, shared much of the blame for his exclusion. Throughout his career, he made few efforts to build bridges to the larger European architectural community; mostly, he appeared content to stand on the sidelines and irritate others with his talks and writings. That he was able to achieve what he did had much more to do with how he related to his friends and acquaintances outside architecture.

Loos's first close friends, when he first moved to Vienna in 1896, were all writers. He was especially close to Peter Altenberg and, even more so, to Karl Kraus. Those he met and spent time with in the first decade of his life in Vienna came almost exclusively from their respective (and combined) circles. Loos met his first wife, Lina Obertimpfler, while spending time with them (at her father's *Gasthaus*, where Altenberg's circle regularly was in attendance). He met his longtime partner, Bessie Bruce, at one of her Cakewalk dance performances, in the company of Altenberg.[34] And when he started to design for clients—first apartments and, later, houses and a few commercial commissions—very nearly all of them were friends or relatives of Kraus, Altenberg, and others they knew.

That pattern would hold for most of the remainder of Loos's life. His friends, acquaintances, and clients would continue to come from outside the architectural world, while his connections with the modernist architects in Vienna and abroad remained tenuous, at best. When Loos experienced one of the great crises of his life, his arrest in 1928 for allegedly molesting three young girls, it was his clients and friends, not his fellow architects, who put up the bail money to release him from prison and who supported him during and after his trial.[35]

Years ago, in the mid-1980s, I had the chance to interview Ernst A. Plischke. He told me something about Loos and his relative isolation I will never forget. When Loos died, Plischke recalled, he left no money for a funeral. Josef Frank, one of the few Viennese modernists at that time who had any enduring connection to Loos, asked Plischke to make the rounds of the city's modernists (at least those who had some sympathy for Loos) to collect money for his burial. The thought had not occurred to anyone else.[36]

6 | Adolf Loos and the Strategies of the *Raumplan*

In 1932, Armand Weiser, editor of the Viennese architectural journal *Die Bau- und Werkkunst*, inserted a correction in the publication's January issue.[1] It came in the form of a brief "response" from Heinrich Kulka, Ludwig Münz, and Franz Glück to a rather negative review Weiser had written the year before of Kulka's book *Adolf Loos: Das Werk des Architekten*.[2]

Münz and Glück had been, as Weiser noted, Kulka's *Helfer*—his helpers or, better, assistants—in the preparation of the work, although neither was credited. All three men were close to Loos. They had either worked for him (which was the case for Kulka), were to some extent friends of his (Münz), or were actively engaged with publishing his writings (Münz and Glück). Some of their joint rebuttal touches on relatively trivial issues, such as the actual title of the book. Weiser had gotten it wrong in his review. There was also the matter of when Loos and Hoffmann had first employed flat roofs for their houses.

The core of their complaint, however, revolved around two questions. The first had to do with whether there was a direct relationship between the *Raumplan* and the ground plan in Loos's thinking (and, indeed, in his buildings). Wiesner had questioned precisely this aspect of Loos's design work, suggesting that Loos's application of the Raumplan was more or less indiscriminate. Kulka, Münz, and Glück were strident in their response. There was, they claimed, an explicit relationship between Loos's conception of the ground plan and how it unfolded spatially.[3] Loos's spatial manipulations were never carried out arbitrarily, they insisted; they arose instead from the plan in a logical and defined way. His system thus was clear-cut and his spatial moves coherent. We will return to this issue.

The second of their "corrections" concerned whether Loos's actual voice was present in the book. According to Kulka, Münz, and Glück, it was, since much of what they had written was based on their interviews of Loos or his frequent impromptu "lectures." Loos was given to long discourses in private or public, laying out his ideas, and all three men had certainly heard him talk at length. They write: "It is not true that 'Loos doesn't speak' in this book and that relatively little is quoted from him. Loos is quoted, though he doesn't speak ... [directly] to the readers." They are saying, in other words, that much of the text that cites Loos's thinking is paraphrase.

The issue at first might appear trivial. It is not. It is particularly important because Kulka's book was the first comprehensive monograph about Loos, and it was the only one that appeared in Loos's lifetime.[4] There are indeed numerous paraphrases of Loos's "thoughts" in the book; in some instances, they offer the only evidence we have of his often-idiosyncratic views. The question remains: How accurate are their retellings of Loos's statements? That is not entirely clear, as Weiser points out. The extent to which we hear (or read) the authentic voice of Loos is in no way certain. In many instances, what Kulka and his coauthors write about the specific aspects of Loos's buildings and projects seems to be drawn from their own observations, not precisely what Loos might have told them.

This question is especially important as it relates to Loos's ideas about spatial planning. The publication of Kulka's book marked the first time his Raumplan concept was discussed in a comprehensive way. Loos had previously offered only a few cryptic lines about his ideas. This had come in 1929, in a footnote of a piece he had written in homage to his favorite cabinetmaker, Josef Veillich, who had died a short time before. Here Loos writes, referring to his absence from the 1927 Stuttgart Weißenhofsiedlung, to which he had pointedly not been invited: "I would have had something to exhibit, namely, the dissolving of the organization of living rooms into space, not on a level surface, story by story, as has been achieved heretofore. With this invention, I would have saved humanity a great deal of work and time in its development."

Loos's statement continues in the footnote: "Because this is the great revolution in architecture: the dissolving of a ground plan into space! Before

Immanuel Kant, people could not think spatially, and architects were forced to make the toilet as high as the formal hall. Only by means of dividing the space in half could they succeed in making lower rooms. And just as we will one day play three-dimensional chess, so other architects will be able in the future to dissolve the ground plan into space."[5]

Aside from these two passages and a few pages in Kulka's 1931 book, nothing else was published concerning the Raumplan during Loos's lifetime. Loos was otherwise silent about his revolutionary concept, and neither the contemporary architectural journals nor the newspapers took much, if any, notice. Even in the many obituaries that appeared after Loos's death, in August 1933, there is scarcely a mention of his revolutionary spatial planning strategies.

Over the next three decades, little else on the subject appeared. It was only with the publication of two works in the early 1960s that the matter again came to the fore. The first of these was an extended essay on Loos written by Kulka and published in the London *Architects' Year Book* in 1960.[6]

By this time, Kulka was living in New Zealand, where he had found refuge after the Nazi takeover of Austria. He had continued his own experiments with the Raumplan, first in Europe (after Loos's death) and, later, after his arrival in New Zealand, in a series of houses constructed in Auckland and elsewhere in the country.[7]

In addition to a brief biography of Loos and a discussion of some of his key theoretical ideas and buildings, Kulka appended a section on "Loos's spatial planning." Here, he presents several important clues and insights. He writes, for example:

> Loos was more acutely aware of the spatial nature of architecture than most architects. He had always been conscious of the following fact: the impression made by the apparent heights and lengths of a room is relative. *Everything is small or large by comparison only.* In his later work he developed to a high degree the ability to plan three-dimensionally or spatially, and made use of the above fact, knowing that a small, low nook, (or recess or annexe), gives the feeling of a mental shelter and appears as a place of contemplation; but *only* if it is part of a larger room; as for example a box at the theatre which by itself would give a feeling of claustrophobia.[8]

Not much is new here; this is largely a restatement of what Kulka had published in his book on Loos in the early 1930s. But Kulka adds:

> The rooms of his houses are situated on various levels, inter-related in harmonious proportions, space flowing into space, but forming a compact unit. The levels are not bound to a special floor (ground floor, first floor, etc.) and are not the result of simply dividing a high room into mezzanine parts. The floors are inter-related rooms with open vistas, the levels connected by steps. These steps are handled in such a natural tactful way, flowing the logical traffic of the house, that the occupants are not aware of the steps and annoyed by them in any way.[9]

The telling statement comes in the last sentence. It implies that Loos was concerned with making the transitions from space to space unobtrusive, and that the occupants should not be aware of the many steps required to go from one place to the next. This is a surprising admission, for it reveals that Loos was cognizant of the impact his complex arrangements might have had on his building's inhabitants. Kulka follows this with another admission, one that seemingly contradicts what he, Münz, and Glück had written in their rejoinder to Weiser: "The houses Loos designed were cubic in their outer appearance, but within the confines of the outer walls, ground and roof, Loos composed his three-dimensional creations freely. The simplicity of the outward appearance is in great contrast to the complex spatial arrangements within."[10]

When Kulka writes that Loos "composed his three-dimensional creations freely" he seems to be reversing his earlier statement about Loos never carrying out his spatial manipulations arbitrarily. In this same section, however, he provides a corrective of sorts:

> Loos never used a raised floor without practical justification; nor without having another room under the raised part. No empty bubbles were allowed. As, according to their function and proportions, smaller rooms require lower heights (dining or library alcoves, baths, cloakrooms, etc. need a mere seven feet [2.13 meters]) and larger rooms require greater height; so Loos worked in these lower alcoves and service rooms contrapuntally against the greater height of the living rooms.
>
> Loos was never a fanatic; he never applied these ideas forcibly; but used this method of spatial planning where he considered it would give the best solution to the building problem.[11]

Loos, Kulka is claiming, made his decisions pragmatically. He was careful in his use of the Raumplan not to waste space, and he applied the idea when he thought it might convey some dividend, either spatial or perceptual.

The last word written by anyone who knew Loos personally came in the second of the two publications from this period, Ludwig Münz and Gustav Künstler's *Der Architekt Adolf Loos: Darstellung seines Schaffens nach Werkgruppen / Chronologisches Werkverzeichnis* (The Architect Adolf Loos: A Presentation of His Works by Building Type / Chronological List of Works), published in 1964.[12] Münz, who wrote some of the key parts of the book, and Künstler, who wrote the remainder, make numerous references to the Loosian Raumplan. One finds such phrases as "durch konsequente Ausnützung eines 'Raumplanes,'' (through the consistent utilization of a Raumplan).[13]

Yet, once again, there are some surprising statements, especially in light of what Münz, Kulka, and Glück had written in their rebuttal in 1932. One is Münz and Künstler's assertion that Loos only came to his full Raumplan conception over time—that it was not until the early 1920s that he had fully developed his scheme. I cite from the English-language version of the book, which appeared two years later:

> The principle of building on a "plan of volumes" [the rather awkward translation of *Raumplan* found throughout the book] did not, of course, suddenly emerge from the brain of its inventor Adolf Loos, but was gradually prepared and clarified—starting with the space that seemed to him the most important for living purposes: the combination without an intermediate wall of a larger, higher room for social gatherings with a smaller, lower one in which to rest or retire.[14]

Münz and Künstler state that this process "seems to have developed according to the laws of strict logic."[15] But precisely what that "strict logic" was they never explain.

If we return to the issue Weiser first raised, about whether Loos followed a rigorous and logical set of rules for the application of the Raumplan, it would seem, considering the later writings of Kulka and Münz, that the truth lies somewhere in the middle. Weiser's contention that Loos's Raumplan was arbitrary is not quite right, but neither is the assertion from Kulka, Münz, and Glück that it arose in a wholly logical and defined way.

To answer the question about how Loos worked, how he carried out his Raumplan strategies, then, a different approach is called for. We cannot rely on the writings—those of Loos or his protégés—because there is not enough substance in them to allow us to make precise judgments. Based on what Loos, Kulka, and Münz and Künstler have written, however, we can assume a few things with some certainty. If what Kulka tells us is correct (which seems very likely), that the initial idea for the Raumplan came to Loos when he was sitting in a theater box, gazing out into an auditorium, that is a significant clue. According to Kulka, Loos observed the interplay between the smaller space and the larger one, and he concluded that having an adjacent, "open" space made a smaller, lower one easier and more pleasant to inhabit.[16]

We also know from Loos himself two other central details: that he believed that the height of a given room should be commensurate with its importance and function, and that space taken from one volume could be reused in another, yielding a certain degree of spatial economy.

We also have evidence from Kulka's 1960 essay that Loos envisioned the Raumplan in another way: that he was concerned with how one would enter and move through a given volume. As I have written elsewhere, Loos, apparently, much like Oskar Strnad and Josef Frank, was interested in how we engage architecture through movement, though our bodily and perceptual interactions with it.[17]

In the end, though, we have little else that sheds light on Loos's thoughts or intentions. It makes no sense to examine Loos's built work or projects looking for some secret, underlying principle of organization (such as a proportional system) because, from the evidence we have, that was not what he was doing. And there are no other texts (barring the miraculous discovery of a long-lost Loos essay or letter) that might illuminate the issue. We are left, thus, to interpret his ideas on the basis of what we can discern in his plans and buildings.

I have identified five strategies that recur with some frequency in Loos's works. There are certainly others. What I discuss below are at least some of the principal ones. How conscious Loos was about applying these ideas is yet another open question: he may have simply carried them out as a matter of course, which is to say they may merely constitute architectural mannerisms—or personal ticks—for him.

Screening

The notion of screening, meaning the rigorous distinction between what was public and private, is present in all Loos's buildings. Loos does this in two ways:

|6.1. Adolf Loos, Villa Müller, Prague, 1928–30, view from the north. Photograph: Martin Gerlach, jun., ca. 1930. Adolf Loos Archiv, Albertina, Vienna, ALA 3199.

through the separation of outside and inside and, in the interior, through what were intended to be entertaining or semi-private versus entirely private spaces.

He achieves the first in the way that has often been remarked upon: with the application of front façades that are essentially "blank." Ofttimes, Loos's street-side elevations are almost forbidding, with fortress-like walls and a relative paucity of windows. His Tristan Tzara House (1925–26) is perhaps the most extreme example of this; but almost all Loos's later Raumplan villas are "closed off" from the street, which is to say from the public. Loos's Villa Müller has a street-side façade that is inaccessible; one has to go around to what is ostensibly the rear to enter the house (fig. 6.1) At times, as in the Rufer House (1922), he

|6.2. Adolf Loos, Rufer House, Vienna, 1922. Photograph: Martin Gerlach, jun., ca. 1930. Adolf Loos Archiv, Albertina, Vienna, ALA 3223.

6.3. Adolf Loos, Steiner House, Vienna, 1910, hall (*Diele*). Photograph: Martin Gerlach, jun., ca. 1930. Adolf Loos Archiv, Albertina, Vienna, ALA 3241.

moved the entry to the side of the building (fig. 6.2); in others, for instance the Scheu House (1912–13) and the project for the Villa Moissi (1923) on the Venice Lido, he raised the entrance well above ground level.

It is in the interiors of his domestic works, though, that Loos effected his other separation of public and private. The idea was not a new one by any means: the houses of the bourgeoisie across Europe and elsewhere in the nineteenth century (and even before) display the same bifurcation between places where guests were received and entertained and the private domain of the occupants. But Loos, through the application of the Raumplan, alters in many respects how these separations are achieved.

In his earliest houses, those completed before World War I, Loos generates this sense of partition in stages. In the Steiner House, for instance, one comes into the house through a tiny vestibule. At this point, the guest would have been first greeted. Beyond, for those who needed to be received and entertained for a brief time, there was the *Diele*, or hall (fig. 6.3). This space could only be reached after someone in the vestibule turned ninety degrees to his or her right, then followed a narrow hall for about four meters, before turning left ninety degrees again to enter this first space. On one side of the room is a small sitting area (arranged in the form of an inglenook), where "casual" guests could be entertained. More "familiar" guests would be led through the Diele to another extended hall that gives access to the salon and dining room at the house's rear.

This "three-stage" arrangement shows up again in the Scheu House. Here, one enters through a vestibule (albeit a great deal larger and lighter than the one in the Steiner House). Beyond is the hall, once more a place set between the fully public and the entirely private spheres. Only after making one's way down another short passage from the hall does one enter the three contiguous rooms—the combined music room and salon, the combined study and inglenook, and the dining room—that form the heart of the home. This was the place where intimate friends and guests were brought and entertained at length.

In both houses, the private areas—the bedrooms and principal bathrooms—are upstairs. The separation in both cases is achieved by a relatively closed staircase (meaning one cannot see directly to the upper floor) leading off the halls.

Loos alters this formula in his later Raumplan houses. In the Rufer House, arguably Loos's first complete Raumplan domestic design, one enters through another tiny vestibule. To the right is a hall and, just beyond, a staircase leading to the main spaces. What is different here, what becomes standard for Loos later in his work, is that the separation between the "zones" is achieved almost exclusively by means of stairways. This even true of the principal living spaces. The main body of the Rufer House is arranged as a set of stacked platforms rotating around a central column. The higher one is in this spatial continuum, the more one achieves privacy, and thus the more exclusive is the space. In this instance, the dining room is afforded views of the lower spaces, yet it is framed in such a way that it has some separation from them (fig. 6.4). The dining room, this "highest space" in terms of its exclusivity, is then connected directly with the stair leading up to the bedrooms.

Over the course of the following decade, Loos would continue to refine his strategies of screening. The Villa Moller's entry sequence is the most extreme example, in as much as the initial entry sequence—the vestibule, hallway, and stair—leading to the first level is so compressed. It is only as one comes to the end of the first flight of stairs that one reaches a small, more open landing. There are also cutouts in the walls that allow views up and through the house (fig. 6.5). Notable release comes only when one climbs the second flight of stairs and enters the main floor, however. Here one finds the two-tiered sitting area, the

|6.4. Adolf Loos, Rufer House, Vienna, 1922, view from the dining room. Photograph: Martin Gerlach, jun., ca. 1930. Adolf Loos Archiv, Albertina, Vienna, ALA 2523.

|6.5. Adolf Loos, Villa Moller, Vienna, 1926–27, view of stair. Photograph: Wolfgang Thaler.

|6.6. Adolf Loos, Villa Müller, Prague, 1928–30, passage facing toward the vestibule and stair. Photograph: Wolfgang Thaler.

salon/music room, and dining room. The sitting area is the perfect expression of Loos's idea of a "graduated" set of spaces, arranged according to their intended privacy. The lower part is less private than the upper; the adjacent salon/music room and dining room provide the areas where the most honored guests would be entertained. Finally, a stair, extending alongside the sitting area, leads up to the bedrooms and bathrooms, the most private domain of the house.

The grand Raumplan villas Loos designed afterward—the Villa Müller (1928–30) and the Villa Winternitz (1930–32), both in Prague, follow similar schemes. The most important difference in the Villa Müller is that the entry sequence is extended—it is twice as long as the one in the Villa Moller—whereas in the Villa Winternitz it is less abrupt, and a great deal more open (figs. 6.6, 6.7).

Compression and Release

Hand in hand with Loos's practice of screening is his imposition of another spatial tactic. One might call it "compression and release," because it is all about placing the viewer first into a very tight, often dark space, before liberating her or him in an adjacent, much larger, and more brilliantly lit space. In the Tristan Tzara House, Loos achieves this by routing the path of access up a long, very nar-

|6.7. Adolf Loos, Villa Winternitz, Prague, 1931–32, vestibule. Photograph: David Cysař.

row winding stairway. Greta Knutson, Tzara's wife, remarked of the stair that "only the cat appreciated" it (fig. 6.8). It extends past a second-level rental apartment and then up a second, winding stair, until one reaches the fourth level of the house, which includes the dining room, salon, and Tzara's atelier.[17] Only here, despite the difference in levels (for the whole floor is effectively bifurcated), does one finally encounter a much greater openness.

Loos's unbuilt house for Josephine Baker in Paris (1927) creates this interplay between compression and release in a different way. The access from the street leads up a grand staircase to the main floor. But all the passageways toward the front of the house, extending around the pool and leading into the café, are narrow and highly compressed. This time, the relaxation comes first, followed by a full sequence of architectonic "squeezing." Much of this is only relieved by the windows looking into the pool, which is set into a double-height volume. The effect is again like Loos's notion of the theater box, looking from a lower, more cramped space into a much larger one to relieve one's sense of confinement.

Loos's Raumplan designs, whether for houses or commercial spaces, all operate in this way: a carefully contrived back-and-forth between what is lower and higher, constricted and open, creates tensions and drama (fig. 6.9).

Control

Control is perhaps the most controversial aspect of Loos's Raumplan. Visitors—and even current residents of his houses—complain that they feel "manipulated" by Loos's spatial sequencing. I heard this most memorably from the head of security at the Villa Moller, which now functions as the Israeli ambassador's house in Vienna. The noted photographer Wolfgang Thaler and I had gone to the villa to photograph it for my *New Space* book. As we gradually ascended through the house, documenting each twist and turn, the thickly muscled security guard carried on an uninterrupted litany of what he thought were the house's many failures, especially the climbing, twisting, and turning that it imposes on the occupant or guest (fig. 6.10). It is difficult, if not impossible, to refute his complaints: the house does continually force one into very specific movements. And the full entry sequence, extending all the way up to the roof deck, is challenging. In places, a charitable person (or architecture aficionado!) might find a certain joy in the experience. Still, the Mossad man had a point: the house is almost beyond demanding.

And the same is true of the Rufer House, the most tightly framed of all Loos's Raumplan villas. After a few steps in any direction, the house compels one to alter course, and the daily patterns of living lead to a very large number of shifts and abrupt turns. Living in the Rufer House requires a high level of athletic prowess.

View Corridors

One of the most arresting aspects of Loos's imposition of moments of compression and release is that along many of his extended pathways are small openings, which afford views to the spaces beyond. Almost never do they offer full release, but they give hints of what is to come. On the one hand, they are promises of an anticipated release; on another, they afford glimpses into the Raumplan system, showing the mechanisms (the placement of walls, windows, larger spaces, corridors, and the interlocking of floors on sundry levels) that underlie the Raumplan and make it work as a spatial conceit.

|6.8. Adolf Loos, House for Tristan Tzara and Greta Knutson, Paris, 1925, stair. From Ludwig Münz and Gustav Künstler, *Der Architekt Adolf Loos: Darstellung seines Schaffens nach Werkgruppen / Chronologisches Werkverzeichnis* (Vienna: Verlag Anton Schroll, 1964), 91.

|6.9. Adolf Loos, Villa Winternitz, Prague, 1931–32, stair to the mezzanine. Photograph: David Cysař.

Resolution

The last aspect of the Loosian Raumplan I want to mention is what I call "resolution." In each of his houses, Loos creates tensions in the viewer/occupant. These can be physical (or somatic), visual, acoustical, or even haptic—or a combination of several or all of these. Yet, even when the houses are at their most confounding, Loos offers moments of respite. Typically, these come in the form of a terminus, a place one reaches after an ascent or a saunter. It may be an inglenook, a sitting space, or an elevated platform, designed for rest and relaxation (fig. 6.11). It is almost as if Loos wished to compensate the subject with a small reward after her or his exertion. In most instances, these places of resolution occur where the space is private, or just at the edge between what is still osten-

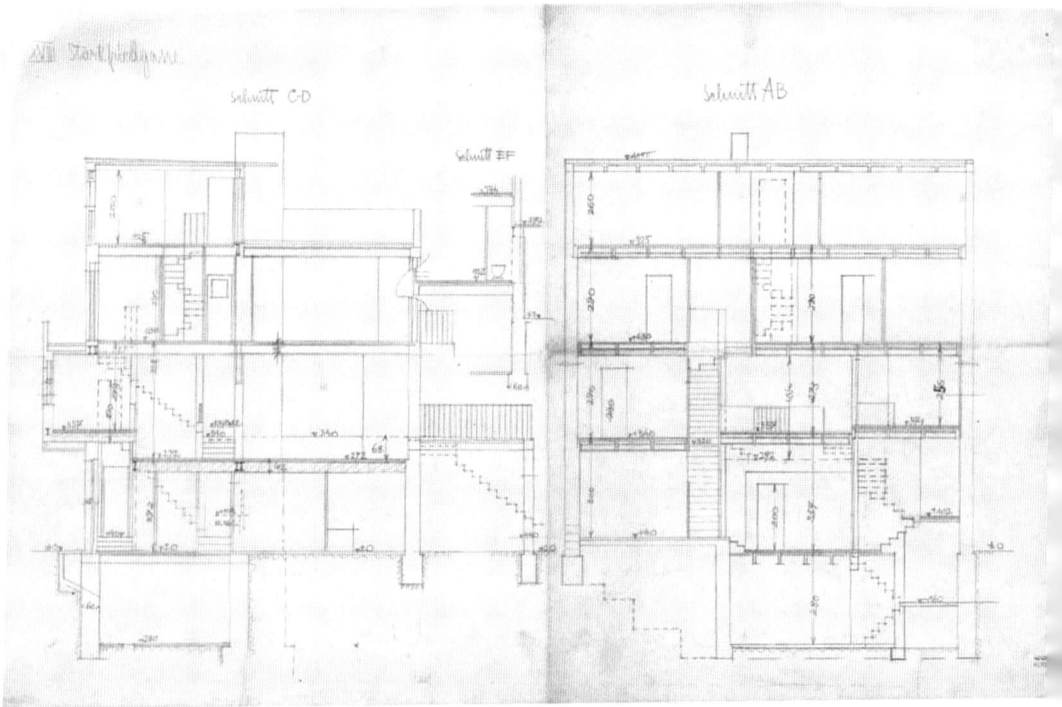

|6.10. Adolf Loos, Villa Moller, Vienna, 1926–27, sections. Adolf Loos Archiv, Albertina, Vienna, ALA 909.

sibly public and private. The sitting entresol of the Villa Winternitz is one example; another is the extended inglenook of the Steiner House.

One could doubtless find many other conceits and examples of Loos's strategies. It is an amusing parlor game. The more interesting question is what it might tell us. The fact that Loos works through a consistent series of themes and variations is evidence on the one hand that what Kulka, Münz, and Glück wrote is true. There is an underlying logic to Loos's Raumplan idea. The same spatial "ticks" occur with regularity, and they follow onto each other in discernable patterns. Yet, at the same time, it is also evident that there is nothing particularly systematic about how Loos frames his spatial journeys and arrangements. It appears, rather, that he was constantly experimenting, trying out new variations or combinations, seeking to find ever better solutions. Other factors also must have played a role in his decisions: site, budget, and the wishes of his clients. These, too, were partly determinative.

|6.11. Adolf Loos, Steiner House, Vienna, 1910, living room. Photograph: Martin Gerlach, jun., ca. 1930. Adolf Loos Archiv, Albertina, Vienna, ALA 3239.

Weiser (who was among the few observers at the time Loos was alive and working to write about the Raumplan) was also correct—and in two ways. He is right to say that the relationship between the ground plan and the unfolding of the Raumplan is not absolute. There are plenty of instances where the two-dimensional and the three-dimensional aspects of Loos's designs do not fully align. And he was correct in writing that there is no perfect logic—no mathematical certitude—embedded in the development of a Loosian Raumplan.

This is all telling. But it is not a final verdict. The Raumplan idea holds onto its power precisely because it is so varied and stimulating. Each house, each sequence is different. Nothing is absolute, nothing is the product of an unassailable logic. What Loos gave us instead are moments—and not a few of them—of great vitality.

7 | Two New Books on Adolf Loos

In a 1968 letter to the Brno art historian Zdeněk Kudělka, Bořivoj Kriegerbeck, who worked with Adolf Loos on several of his late projects, wrote of his first meeting with Loos. It was the spring of 1928. "I was employed by the large construction company Müller and Kapsa, and our offices were on the ground floor of two large buildings, where Loos's last father-in-law Josef [actually Otto] Beck lived on the second floor. ... One day around noon, when I was the only one there, Loos came by our office with an inartistic hand-drawn sketch on a scrap cut from a large bag of flour and asked me to draw it to scale. I did it for him, and he remained faithful to me ever after."[1]

Kriegerbeck would go on to work—to varying degrees—on Loos's interiors for his clients in Pilsen, including the apartment of Otto Beck, the late, unfinished apartment for Oskar Semmler, as well as several small unbuilt *Raumplan* houses. Most importantly, he worked with Loos on the Villa Müller in Prague. The letter cited above was only one of several writings by Kriegerbeck that have been collected by museums and archives in the Czech Republic: the City of Prague Museum, the Brno City Archives, and Brno University of Technology's Faculty of Fine Arts. The documents include texts written by Kriegerbeck at three different times, the so-called "Diaries I and II," dating from the period

1928 to 1933; the "Bedside Talks" from 1930; and the "Notes" Kriegerbeck put together in the late 1960s and 1970s. Kudělka, who spent many years studying Loos's life and work, was instrumental in helping the various institutions acquire these documents.[2]

Recently, a team of scholars in Brno and Pilsen, Jindřich Chatrný, Dagmar Černoušková, Jana Kořínková, and Karel Zoch, assembled these writings and published them as a book, along with an extensive commentary. For the past three decades, very much of the most interesting and original research on Adolf Loos has come from Czech scholars; this volume in no exception.

What emerges from Kriegerbeck's accounts is a vivid portrait of Loos in his last years. We see Loos at work—and his unusual working methods. Through Kriegerbeck, we also hear something of Loos's ideas in those years. Most movingly, perhaps, we see Loos, the man, in his final days, with his full personality on display—those moments when he was kindly and thoughtful, but also the times when he was petty, arrogant, and irksome.

Kriegerbeck also tells us about Loos's Pilsen clients, most importantly, perhaps, how they came to him. "Loos was first brought to Pilsen by Josef [Otto] Beck, and the first interior that he did was for the factory owner Willy Hirsch. That was in 1907. [I]n the spring of 1928," he continues,

> [w]hen the factory owner [Otto] Beck moved out of the [rental] apartment [where he had been living], the same flat was furnished for Dr. Josef Vogl. After this, other interiors just came pouring in.
>
> You see, it was like this: All those clients were Jews, and very rich ones at that. They formed a closed society amongst themselves. In addition, they were roughly the same age, around 30–40. The men were obsessed with business, and they did not pay much attention to their wives, who, being bored, took up decorating their homes. If Mrs. Hirsch had something, then Mrs. Semler did, too, and Mrs. Vogl, and so on.[3]

Kriegerbeck is mostly gentle and respectful when writing about Loos. In one especially sweet passage, he writes:

> Those who had the good fortune to be close to him or even to work with him can pass pleasant hours of their lives telling stories and pleas-

> ant memories of Adolf Loos. Adolf Loos was a cauldron filled with a universal content. He knew everything and you could speak with him about it all. He was jovial, loving, direct, and did not hide his opinions. He expressed himself politely. He was neither arrogant nor conceited. You could turn to him for anything, and he always explained things, offered advice, or tried to help, which made working with him and for him so beautiful. He always knew what he wanted and never improvised. Loos was deaf. In the beginning, we talked to him loudly, later with the help of a hearing aid, and in his final years he couldn't hear even with a hearing aid. We wrote our questions on a board, using just key words. Loos was very witty and understood things easily, so he quickly grasped what we wanted, what we were asking about. Perhaps nature itself arranged it so that what he lost in hearing he gained in vision. His vision was piercing; nothing escaped him. He saw every improper millimeter, every discrepancy in colors or improper material. And he possessed this great sense not just as a person for people, but also for matter, for the materials used. That is why he used beautiful wood, stone, leather, etc. This was the source of his statement that ruining wood by cutting it and stone by carving it was a crime, thus also his aversion to ornament.[4]

We also see another side of Loos. Kriegerbeck remembers the day in the summer of 1931, when he went to visit Loos at the St. Margarete Spa near Prachatice, in south Bohemia. There he also saw Loos's third (and last) wife, Claire (Klara) Beck Loos. (Loos called her "Lerle.") The couple had been having problems for some time; their marriage would end in divorce, just as Loos's two prior ones had.[5] At one point, Claire beckoned Kriegerbeck into the bedroom. He remembered that she "took off her clothes and underwear and showed me the bruises from where Loos had beat her."[6]

This and other similar revelations into Loos's character are disturbing. But Kriegerbeck reveals important information about Loos's practice too. One passage explains a detail of the Villa Müller that had long puzzled observers. "Loos enjoyed placing some small humorous element in each of his interiors, something he called a "lark." He'd gotten it into his head to place an aquarium inside a marble half wall, on the side facing the dining room. He told me how it would stand out, especially in the evening, if the aquarium was lit from all sides." Kriegerbeck took Loos to "a co-op of small-scale aquarists" and left him there while he did some other shopping. When he returned "about an hour later," he found Loos "going from aquarium to aquarium, overjoyed and downright obsessed. He took a childlike pleasure from it all."[7]

Another of Kriegerbeck's anecdotes reveals Loos's attitudes to modernism—or better, his aversion to what was then in the mainstream. Walking with Loos and Claire across Wenceslas Square one evening, they stopped. Loos, who by that time had trouble walking, was exhausted and needed a rest. Loos, Kriegerbeck remembered, "took my hand and said, 'What do you think of that Baťa building?' 'I like it.' To which he replied: Please! What do you see in it? It is just a 'Luftschacht' [ventilation shaft]" (fig. 7.1).[8]

It is Kriegerbeck's fine-grained descriptions of working with Loos—and Loos's peculiar working methods—that are the most illuminating, however: "When Loos did something, he had it all thought out in advance—in his head, as he put it. He literally saw the thing in his mind, he walked through that home as if it had already been finished; he just needed someone to, in his words, put it on paper for him. He neither experimented nor improvised."[9]

Both oddities—that Loos didn't (or rarely) drew and that he worked out his designs in advance and refused to alter them—created innumerable problems. Loos's verbal instructions, for one, were not always clear. Karel Lhota, who produced the initial renderings for the Villa Müller, made several errors in the structure and the heights of spaces (something that Loos's complex Raumplan scheme only exacerbated), and the plans had to be redrawn. Loos also forced contractors to make expensive and time-wasting changes if they deviated even slightly from what he had specified. And he was often away from the building sites—sometimes for weeks on end—meaning that crucial decisions were delayed or made in Loos's absence, only to be "corrected" when he appeared again. During the design and construction of the Villa Müller, Loos was often in Vienna, dealing with the repercussions of his divorce from Claire and his trial on charges of having molested three young girls there.[10] (Kriegerbeck specifically notes that he believed Loos to be innocent. He also notes that Dr. František Müller, his employer and Loos's client for the house, told him that the accusations were trumped up and political in nature.[11])

Through it all, Kriegerbeck worked patiently with Loos, doing all he could to help bring the villa to completion. And despite the assertions of Heinrich Kulka—another of Loos's assistants—that Loos designed the house in collaboration with Karel Lhota, Kriegerbeck is unequivocal: "I must declare with my best knowledge and conscience that the entire villa is Loos's spiritual creation."[12] This is perhaps the largest payoff from the book: Kriegerbeck was convinced,

|7.1. Jindřich Svoboda, František Lydie Gahura, Josef Gočár, and Arnošt Sehnal, Baťa Store, Prague, 1927–28. Private collection.

despite Loos's many absences, his declining health, his poor hearing, his unwillingness or inability to draw, and his often mercurial manner, that the Villa Müller (and by extension, one has to assume, all his late works) were thoroughly and uniquely his own, and not the products of his assistants, as some have suggested. Somehow, Loos was able to work effectively with others to achieve his aims.

Kriegerbeck is certainly correct here. For anyone steeped in Loos's work, his distinctive hand shows through in all his late works. It is not only the unique spatial ordering or the idiosyncratic handling of the façades: it is the complete package, the idea of living and Central European bourgeois culture that is so present, so consistent. And even where Loos was not fully responsible—for example, in the interiors of the Villa Winternitz in Prague, which were Lhota's, Loos's spirit is manifest everywhere. Lhota and the contractors they used were so steeped in Loos's aesthetic that they could hardly have done otherwise.[13]

Recently, three members of the same team that put out the Kriegerbeck memoir, Chatrný, Černoušková, and Kořínková, produced a large exhibition catalogue, *Evropan Adolf Loos, Nejen brněnske stopy / Adolf Loos, European: His Legacy in Brno and Beyond*, which accompanied a show by the same name held at Špilberk Castle in Brno in the second half of 2020.[14] The text contains fifteen essays, all the work of Czech and Austrian authors. Most of the essays, as the book's title suggests, are focused on Loos's connections to his hometown of Brno. There are very good essays on Loos's father, the sculptor Adolf Loos Sr., by Pavla Cenková; on Loos's first house design in Brno for Karl (Karel) Herold, by Černoušková and Chatrný; on the house Loos designed at the sugar refinery in Hrušovany u Brna, by Kořínková and Černoušková; and on the renovation of the old chateau for Viktor Bauer in Brno, by Kořínková. Two Austrian authors, Claudia Lang-Auinger and the late Iris Meder, also contributed pieces. Lang-Auinger wrote on Loos and antiquity; Meder wrote about the House for Paul and Marietta Himmelreich, designed by two of Loos's students, Karl Hoffmann and Felix Augenfeld.

The editors also reproduced two essays by Kudělka, the Brno-based scholar perhaps more responsible than any other for inaugurating and carrying out the Loos revival in the Czech lands over nearly half a century, from around 1950 till the time of his death in 2000.[15] Kudělka was passionate—better, inexorable—in his pursuit of Loos's legacy, and it is particularly fitting that his voice is present here.

It was not only that Kudělka spent decades collecting every document, every scrap of information, every trace of Loos in the Czech lands he could ferret out; he was also remarkably perceptive about Loos's ideas and how they were expressed in his work. One of the pieces reproduced in the catalogue is an excerpt from an essay Kudělka wrote on Loos's conception of "living space" in 1983.[16] Even in fragmentary form, the brilliance of Kudělka's analysis shines through. He was the first, I believe, to notice something that was central to Loos's Raumplan idea: "Loos," he writes, "endeavored to create a horizontally as well as a vertically continuous spatial core" in his houses.[17] In other words, one of the essential elements of the Raumplan is that the two conditions—walking on a level surface and moving either up or down through the interlinked volumes set on different levels—were both part of the same conception for Loos: that in a given volume one would embark on an extended journey and that all parts of that journey belonged to the same experience. One portion of the journey was not in any way set off from the other.

Kudělka also recognized that in Loosian space there are always elements of continuity—continuous space—alongside marked division, or closed space.[18] Loos was always deliberate in the ways in which he set out his spaces. They are visibly demarcated, regular in their way, and often set in alignment, be it axial or some other form. Yet one's experience of these spaces is highly varied and complex, even while they are still somehow reassuring. Kudělka again: "Loos thus created an environment in which a person could realize all modes of his natural relationships to space and that also protected him through its concentrated organization."[19]

The purpose of all this was not only to "save space" by transferring it to a more important room from a less important one. This notion of spatial economy was Loos's only stated rationale for the Raumplan.[20] What Kudělka saw, more plainly than any other commentator of his time (except perhaps Julius Posener), was that Loos's spatial ordering was closely bound up with the rituals and practices of daily life. It was not merely a conceit Loos imposed to force a certain kind of engagement with his buildings; much more, it was a way of enriching what was already present in Central European bourgeois life:

> For Loos, the inhabited space was not merely a place to be or to find oneself in, a sort of indifferent medium ruled only by physical qualities; it was an environment full of meanings that refer to the main functions of the dwelling-home. One example of this is the space's time-neutralizing function, which lifts the home out of the flow of time in order to essentially eternalize it; another is ceremony, by which the dwelling escapes everyday routine and challenges us to engage in encounters, making them festive elements despite their almost regular repetition. At the top of this hierarchy of meaning was, without a doubt, this invitation for all members of the family to meet and linger in the dwelling's spatial core. Within this hierarchy, Loos placed the family members' sense of belonging to the family—that pluralist entity that was his main focus when contemplating the form of a dwelling-home—above their ability to isolate themselves from one another. Loos's conception of the living space was thus based on the notion of the family as the foundation of modern society and on the space's importance for the family's private and social life.[21]

Seen in this way, Loos's idea of the Raumplan becomes something else altogether. It is not merely a tactic to save space or a parlor trick to amaze or titillate. It is a means instead to guide one in one's daily life, to give meaning, and to allow for social interaction. Loos here suddenly becomes the quintessential humanist.

Kudělka's piece is special. But there is so much more that is excellent and insightful in this catalogue. Some of the revelations are the product of diligent, hands-on research (the sort of historical research that leads to one's fingers becoming etched with dust, which, alas, is becoming much less common today). One of the discoveries Kořínková and Černoušková made, for example, concerns the design and building of Loos's 1914 house for the Brno industrialist Viktor Ritter von Bauer-Rohrfelden at the sugar refinery he owned in Hrušovany u Brna (at the time called Rohrbach) in southern Moravia. What was known about the house previously was fragmentary. Kořínková and Černoušková have assembled a veritable trove of information, every document, photograph, and anecdote concerning the house one could imagine. Most importantly, they give at least a partial answer to one of the longstanding questions about the house—namely, whether Loos contributed in any way to its interiors. Kudělka thought so, based on a photograph showing what he believed to be the uncompleted dining room. That image turned out to be a photo of Bauer's chateau in Brno. The two authors, however, did find a photograph made around 1930 (the only one to come to light) of the house's vestibule and stairs, which "shows clear signs of Loos's touch."[22] So Loos may have at least completed a few interior spaces.

Equally impressive is Černoušková's article on the rooftop penthouse Loos designed for Heinrich Jordan in 1931. It was Loos's last project in Brno. The drawings were made by Loos's assistant Kurt Unger, who, in a later letter to Kudělka, wrote that the design was only "preliminary." In fact, as the plans of the three-floor flat published in the book demonstrate, Loos and Unger had worked it out in some detail. Jordan, in a letter also reproduced in the catalogue in facsimile, expresses his complete dissatisfaction with the proposed design. Loos responded angrily that he was surprised that Jordan would reject it after their discussions about the design.

The takeaway here is something that seems to be consistent in Loos's later years (and perhaps even in his earlier career): he was not a very good listener. That might come off as a bad joke about a man who was already profoundly deaf. The point is that Loos seemed to "talk over" many of his clients, giving them what he thought they needed rather than what they truly wanted. Loos was not the only modernist architect in this club. The acting president had to have been Frank Lloyd Wright, who was famous for belittling his clients' wishes and blithely overriding them. In Loos's case, though, it does tell us something: that client input probably had little to do with the variations in his Raumplan designs, that Loos's own "imperatives" were more likely determinative.

I want to touch on just one other piece (though all in the catalogue are deserving of discussion): Iris Meder's article on the house that Hoffmann and Augenfeld, both protégés of Loos and students from his private *Bauschule*, built for the Himmelreich family in Brno in the early 1930s. Meder sadly died all too young of pancreatic cancer; this was one of the last of her scholarly endeavors. It was difficult for me to read now because I knew her well, and I know how talented she was and how palpable was her joie de vivre.

The question Meder raises is how much the two architects took over from Loos. Or, more pointedly, how Loosian is the house's design? The exterior shows almost no traces of Loos. It is a conventional, rectangular block, with mostly symmetrical fenestration and a standard hipped roof. To my eye, the only feature that looks at all like something that might have come from Loos's hand is the stair-stepped railing leading to the main floor and terrace. Inside, the ground floor exhibits some elements of the Raumplan. There is Loos's typical separation of service and living spaces, and there are small differences in the heights of the floors. But there is none of the openness that Loos's later villas show; the rooms are tightly contained, with few opportunities for continuous views and little interaction between the principal public rooms.

This is less a commentary on Hoffmann and Augenfeld's abilities (the house is lovely and livable in its way) than it is a powerful testimony to the originality and power of what Loos was doing in the last decade of his life. By comparison, the work of these students appears timid.

Taken together, these two books are proof of what can be accomplished with dogged research and intelligent analysis. They are refreshingly free of jargon, free of the need to look trendy or overly clever. We see very good professional historians working professionally—adeptly, perceptively. What we get is a view of the past that is more nuanced and more complete. Loos appears in all his many guises. He is complex—at times brilliant, at times foolish, petulant and kindly, sagacious and childish, filled with his own convictions and also occasionally in some doubt. He is a far more interesting figure for all that.

8 | Adolf Loos, We Hardly Knew Ye: An Obituary

"Johnny I Hardly Knew Ye" was popular song in Britain and Ireland in the nineteenth century. First published in London in 1867, it was reportedly composed by Joseph B. Geohegan, a prolific English songwriter and music-hall celebrity of the day. The song had a long afterlife, borrowed or recast for an array of other songs, from "When Johnny Comes Marching Home," the American Civil War ballad, to "The English Civil War," by The Clash. But the song's origins extend at least five decades further back from the time it supposedly first appeared, to the early nineteenth century or slightly before, when, it is now believed, it was composed in Ireland as an anti-recruiting song, in response to the Kandyan Wars, fought in Sri Lanka from 1795 to 1818. It was originally a farewell or lament. Over time, "I hardly knew ye" became a witty retort to questions about someone who had been long been absent.[1]

Both these senses—as well as the literal one, that one had simply passed away without leaving much of a trace—are in play in a short obituary of Adolf Loos that appeared in the *Architect & Building News* in October 1933.[2]

Published in London, the *Architect & Building News* at that time was the leading professional architectural journal in the United Kingdom. It was widely read throughout the English-speaking world, especially in the United States. I reproduce the obituary here in its totality because what it says about Loos, his life, and his import tells us much about how he was viewed abroad at the time.

> The death of Adolf Loos marks the passing of one of the most significant architects of our time, one who has never received the full credit for the great contribution he made to the progress of architecture in this century.
>
> Thirty years ago, Loos was working almost as a lone hand and laying the foundations of much for which some architects in Europe with a greater sense of publicity have claimed the credit. Loos stands easily first among the exponents of modernism in architecture; but he differed from many, in so far that he had a very great sense of quality, and appreciation and understanding of fine materials. He never "stunted," and was one of the first to shun the word "modern" in describing his work, aiming, as he always did, at the rational rather than the fashionable.
>
> Some of his work, carried out even as far back as thirty years ago, is as advanced as much of what is being done to-day in Europe. Most of his interiors are severe in their simplicity but have a richness in quality due to a careful and knowledgeable selection of good materials, which is often absent to-day.
>
> The Kärntner Bar is Vienna is an outstanding example of Loos' ingenuity. It was opened in 1907, and since then no change whatever has been made, nor has it needed redecoration. The average person, seeing it for the first time, always gets the impression that it is one of the latest of the many "snappy" bars with which Vienna abounds.
>
> Loos was born in Berne [*sic*] in 1870, his father being a monumental sculptor. He started his architectural studies in Vienna, where he worked for a year, afterwards going to Dresden to the technical high school. He never finished his course, but went to America, where he worked for a time as a designer in a chair factory. Later, when out of a job as an architectural assistant, he worked as a bricklayer in order to keep himself. Later he returned to Vienna and started to practice. Amongst others who worked in his office was Le Corbusier.

> He built quite a number of private houses and other buildings in Vienna during the time he was practicing there, all of which stand to-day "fresh and undated."
>
> His later years he spent in Paris, where he died at the age of sixty-three, from paralysis. Loos was an extremely interesting personality, often forceful and almost embarrassing in the expression of his opinions, but underneath a most delightful man.[3]

The piece is signed at the end "F.R.Y." This no doubt refers to the British architect, writer, and painter Maxwell Fry. Fry was certainly in a position to know something about Loos. Born in 1899, he belonged to the generation of British modernists that emerged after World War I. He was trained at Liverpool University in the architectonic language of late imperial neoclassicism, which persisted in Britain long after it had disappeared in most other European countries. He eventually shed all that, and for a time, during the 1930s, he practiced with Walter Gropius in London (during Gropius's short-lived stay in Britain before he immigrated to the United States). Later, in the early 1950s, he worked alongside Le Corbusier and Pierre Jeanneret on the plans for the new Indian city of Chandigarh.

Given his impressive modernist pedigree, the first question one must ask is, Why did he get so much wrong about Loos? It is a longish list: Loos's place of birth (Brno or Brünn, not Berne[4]); where he studied architecture (never in Vienna, first in Brno, at the Staatsgewerbeschule, or State Trades School, then in Dresden, at the polytechnic); and what he did in America (there is no evidence that Loos ever worked in a chair factory or as a bricklayer). The biggest howler of all, however, is Fry's assertion that Le Corbusier worked in his office (quite beyond the fact that Loos never had "an office" in the usual sense, Le Corbusier worked in Berlin for Peter Behrens before World War I, not in Vienna and never for Loos). And Loos didn't die in Paris; his last years were spent in Czechoslovakia and Austria. He died at a sanatorium in Kalksburg, just outside Vienna, and the cause of his death was probably a series of strokes.

Fry's comment that Loos was "underneath a most delightful man" implies that he must have met him at some point. Most likely, this happened in Paris in the later 1920s. That he also notes that Loos was "often forceful and almost embarrassing in the expression of his opinions" suggests further that he may have had a discussion or discussions with Loos. It is certainly an apt description of how Loos expressed his views.

Anyone who writes very much and for a long time, as Fry did, will inevitably commit at least a few errors. Pointing them out is usually the dominion of pedants—especially those who write little but pride themselves on finding the mistakes of others. That is not my purpose at all. Here, the near tsunami of things that are wrong tells us more about Loos than it does about Fry; namely, that in 1933 so little had been written about Loos (especially in English) that Fry could find almost no reliable information. He must have based his account on what he found in Kulka's book *Adolf Loos: Das Werk des Architekten* (in the printed obituary, Fry reproduces a portrait of Loos and a photograph of the Kärntner Bar, both taken from Kulka's work, but he may not have been able to read the German text), his own scant knowledge, and hearsay.[5]

Where Fry is mostly spot-on is in his assessment of Loos's significance. At times, he truly insightful. When he writes that Loos "differed from many, in so far that he had a very great sense of quality, and appreciation and understanding of fine materials," he goes to the essence of what Loos held most dear. In same way, his assertion that Loos was "one of the first to shun the word 'modern' in describing his work, aiming, as he always did, at the rational rather than the fashionable" is a clear-eyed understanding of Loos's efforts. Where he misses badly is in his statement that Loos's "interiors are severe in their simplicity." Hardly. And certainly not compared with the emerging "functionalist" minimalism of the 1920s and early 1930s.

Still, Fry recognized Loos's prescience as an architect at a time when many, if not most, commentators were stuck on Loos's supposed repudiation of all ornament. (Loos, it should be said, never shunned ornament per se, but rather the efforts of the modernists to create and employ new ornament.) And Fry was willing to concede what many others were not: that Loos's modernism still retained validity, that it might yet offer lessons for the future.

The obvious omission in this short remembrance, however, repeats what one can find in almost every obituary written about Loos in that time: there was little, if any, mention—much less an appreciation—of Loos's *Raumplan* idea, his reframing of concepts about space and space-making. Why Fry, an architect with a good eye and a sharp mind, missed something so epochal is hard to explain. If it is correct that he possessed a copy of Kulka's book (or at least had seen one), he must have come away with some impression of what Loos was doing. Anyone with a basic understanding of architecture can see in the drawings and photographs a way of making space that was new and powerful. Could Fry really have missed it? Many, if not most, of the other obituaries of Loos were written by journalists and appeared in the newspapers. They were more interested in Loos's scandals and his outrageous statements than his work. To the extent that they wrote much at all about his achievements, they focused on his war on ornament. But Fry was writing for architects, in a leading architectural journal. He must have known what he was seeing in Loos's works.

There are only a few possible explanations: Fry observed Loos's Raumplan idea and discounted it. Or Fry observed Loos's Raumplan idea and thought it would be of no interest to English-speaking readers—that it was too arcane, too "Continental." Or Fry observed Loos's Raumplan idea and thought it had no real future, so why mention it? Or Fry was simply too fixated on "surfaces," materials, and style and overlooked what was staring him in the face. I suspect the last is what happened. The few comments relating to form that Fry does make in his piece all have to do with the "superficial" aspects of Loos's architecture.

In that, he was not much different from most other commentators of the day. The constant refrain about Loos's assault on ornament, his cultural crusade, and his prescient modernity almost completely drowned out any acknowledgment of the most important thing he had realized as an *architect*: fostering a novel and potent idea of space-making.

Adolf Loos, We Hardly Knew Ye—or your greatest accomplishment.

Appendix

Adolf Loos 1870–1933: A Lecture, by Julius Posener

Originally published as Julius Posener, *Adolf Loos 1870–1933: Ein Vortrag* (Berlin: Akademie der Künste, 1984).

It is not without embarrassment that I speak to you about Adolf Loos. Dietrich Worbs, who planned this exhibition and mounted it with the aid of his coworkers here in the Berlin Academy of Arts, should have been the one to give this talk.[1] When it comes to Loos, I am his student. But it is customary in this institution that exhibitions are formally opened by a member; and that I am the one to do so has its merits, insofar as I can better praise Dietrich Worbs's long and devoted engagement with the works of Adolf Loos than he himself could.

Like everyone who deals with Loos, Worbs faced the challenge of hacking through the undergrowth of myths and legends that pervade Loos's works and writings. Seen from the German viewpoint, Loos launched his assault on ornament too early, because the rejection of ornament belonged to the later development of modern architecture. To be sure, before the First World War, people were already speaking about simplicity; but they were referring to the simplicity of the period around 1800. They were reacting to the superfluity of the *Gründerjahre,*[2] and there was a desire to return to good old-fashioned handcraft, the pride of erecting a well-built wall, a light, solid, and elegantly joined window, a robust roof. One can still find these virtuous features in the most modern buildings from the time just before the war: Peter Behrens's factory buildings are not handcrafted, but in their engineered look we can find the same detailing, the same objective realism. It only becomes clear how shocking Loos's designs were if one compares Behrens's works with the street-front façade of Loos's Steiner House in Vienna. Loos stripped away everything of what in those days was considered the expression of structure, because architects then were still fixated on the building art of earlier times; but he also stripped away any sense of what was called handicraft and, moreover, what one could call representation. He left nothing but a bare façade, with holes cut into it. For his contemporaries, it was pure impertinence, exactly as Loos wanted it to be. Loos belonged to that constellation of important Viennese—Karl Kraus was another of them—who could not have cared less if other people were offended. The bleakness of his façades was unconditional.

At the turn of the century, there was not yet an aesthetic device to soften his façades. It was not until around the middle of the 1920s that architects began to learn how to deal with abstract masses and surfaces, to merge them together into compositions. Adolf Loos did not achieve that before the war, and he didn't do it later, either: he was one of the few architects whom the form canon of the De Stijl movement bypassed, without leaving a trace in his work, just as had been the case with the Secession style, which had developed into such a mighty presence in Austria. It, too, left no mark on his work. The preeminent architects of the 1920s had no more a sense of how even to begin to respond to his work than the leading architects of the prewar era. But they came up with a catchphrase with which they sought to describe this bothersome architect, to somehow make him fit into the recent development of architecture: he became a "forerunner." Loos was no forerunner, though, because he did not want to go where the architecture of the 1920s went. For them, he became a stepping stone on the path to the new architecture. In truth, he was something else altogether.

You can see then how difficult it is to understand this architecture. To mention one other episode—it belongs to his struggle against ornament—the drama surrounding his Haus am Michaelerplatz. The Viennese rejected it, they demanded a different design from another architect, and, in the end, they forced Loos—at a minimum—to add window boxes beneath the windows on the upper stories.

Loos suffered mightily from this rejection—to the point where he had a nervous breakdown. Yet, if one stands before the Haus am Michaelerplatz today, it requires effort to grasp why it was the subject of so much controversy. One sees only an elegant edifice. To be sure, the façade of the stories above the mezzanine level is bare, with window apertures cut into it, in keeping with Loos's usual practice; but the ground floor and mezzanine levels are handled in a traditional architectonic fashion, in the most tried and true sense; we see columns and an entablature—albeit a highly reduced one—in the most classical way; and, if the "bay windows" on the mezzanine seems strange in this context—and disturbing—we have to consider the long historical epoch and the dominant taste leading up to that moment to discover what was shocking about this elegant and groundbreaking structure; but that is not really possible anymore, because what impresses us now is its harmoniousness. You would have to think like a historicist to perceive its strangeness, what was shocking and unique about it, how this work of Adolf Loos appeared in its time—in their time. A certain strangeness does make sense: Loos belonged neither to the epoch in which his design came to fruition nor to the earlier one. He remained apart from the ideals of the avant-garde of the years before 1914 just as he kept his distance from the ideals of the avant-garde before 1933. And certainly, he stayed away from the reactionaries of both epochs. If he felt—with a despair bordering on complacency—that he was a stranger in his time, a being sui generis, a man of a time yet to come, he was right: he was a being sui generis, a man of a time yet to come. Whether he was indeed a man of a time yet to come is something that those, like Dietrich Worbs, who is very much engaged with the questions of his importance for our time and the unfulfilled promise of his architecture, will have to decide.

These questions, ladies and gentlemen, are some of the difficulties standing in the way of people like Dietrich Worbs when they think about Loos. Over the course of the last ten years, I have had the privilege—and the pleasure—to observe him on his path toward understanding and to accompany him along the way. Our most recent interaction—in *nomine Loosi*—is, of course, the present exhibition. Worbs asked me to write an essay for the catalogue, which arose almost effortlessly from our frequent discussions. Loos, according to Worbs's thesis, placed the *Raumplan* at the center of his work. The Raumplan breaks through the floors of a building. It is a way of planning that assigns to each room its individual height, the height differing between rooms, some of which, though they are on sundry levels, are connected to each other, while others are set off to themselves. Even these rooms have their own specific positions in the arrangement. This is the reason why stairs—or different sets of stairs—take on a special importance. The stairs cut through and expose the sundry levels of the house; the way they are lit offers an invitation to those entering to climb upward; and the dark zones can function like a pause in music. Not only the stairs, but also all the paths through the house take on a new meaning. This concept, without question, occupies a central place in Loos's thinking. In our discussions about the Raumplan, I took the position that aspects of this notion [of spatial planning] had to have preceded that of Loos and his contemporaries, because anyone, I insisted, who develops a new way of thinking only takes it forward a single step; and those who come after him will take it one step further. Worbs was receptive to this argument, and he suggested that I write a piece for the exhibition catalogue, pointing out to me those forerunners and contemporaries of Loos in whose work aspects of the Raumplan were very likely to be found. The results of my research astonished even me; I discovered, to be sure, that in works of Richard Norman Shaw, in England, and some of his contemporaries and followers, and similarly in those of the Henry Hobson Richardson and his followers in the United States, initial approaches to spatial planning that Loos developed into a concept, but only the first glimmers of the idea. I discovered that an older contemporary of Loos, Hermann Muthesius, had fully developed a notion of paths leading through a house with stairs serving to reveal the way; but once more, this idea of setting out paths was still a long way from the way in which Loos conceived of the Raumplan. I had to admit that I was mistaken. Loos had not just made a single step forward: the Raumplan was rightly entirely his. He also applied his concept to commercial buildings, like that of the men's outfitters Goldman & Salatsch on Michaelerplatz; and he pursued it not only in his many projects for apartment buildings, but also the series of villas he built, one after another—all of which one must interpret as realizations of the Raumplan.

When I was finishing the essay, I had a suspicion that Worbs had presented me with student homework, because he already knew the answer and wanted me to undertake the exercise, so that I would recognize it as well. This exhibition, in any case, offers conclusive evidence that the Raumplan, the evidence of which appears very early in Loos's work, was further developed, refined, and, finally, brought to perfection as he developed it, that it gave space to a new freedom, and new importance—and, as odd as it might sound in this context—gave it economy, so much so, that the last little house he designed (it is known as "The Last

House") looks very nearly like a magic trick. Worbs presented his evidence, not only by showing photographs of the spaces that have never been seen, or in sizes much larger than in the books where they had appeared (which was equally revealing), but also by exhibiting two models of each house: one in the scale of 1:50, showing the overall exterior form of the structure, and a second one, in the scale of 1:33, providing insight into the houses' spatial dispositions. These wonderful models—many of them built by Friedrich Kurrent's students in Munich, who became ever more inspired as they worked—are, in my opinion, the centerpiece of the exhibition, an exhibition, ladies and gentlemen, for which one must take some time, and of which one will have the sense that a single visit does not fully exhaust the possibilities. It is an exhibition—and this one can say without exaggeration—that reveals a new picture of Adolf Loos.

One would think that Loos would have commented on the Raumplan on multiple occasions, for we know that he was a prolific writer. But there is only a single instance when he did so, in the obituary he wrote about his cabinetmaker, Josef Veillich.[3] From his earliest days, he was an architect who wrote; one might even say that he was an art journalist. There is hardly a matter related to the broader fields of applied art and architecture about which he did not take a polemical position. It was always polemical, for even when he issued praise, he also admonished those whose shared his outlook—for instance, Hofrat von Scala, the new museum director, who exhibited [Loos's beloved] English furniture. The title of the journal he published—which he wrote entirely by himself and which soon went under—was equally polemical: he called it *Das Andere, ein Blatt zur Einführung der abendländischen Kultur in Österreich* (The other, a magazine for the introduction of Western culture into Austria). In keeping with this effort to expose everything that was false, to show what was truly happening, and to make clear to anyone with a healthy dose of common sense what was good and correct, he wrote about everything that was pertinent to his time: about the way in which one should live, how one should dress, how one should build housing estates, how one should make furniture, what a proper cigarette case is, what modern art is and what it is not, about the tyranny of an art that reached into all aspects of everyday life and felt entitled to do so, what the Secession was doing, and also the German Werkbund (he rejected both)—in a word, about everything; and he did so in way that was always provocative, always readable, always personal, and not infrequently satirical, in the mode of Aristophanes: the story of "Von einem armen reichen Mann" (The poor rich man) one readily can recite verbatim.[4] Only when it came to the Raumplan did he have little to say, he simply built it. He certainly did not endorse the saying, "Bilde, Künstler, rede nicht!" (Create artist, do not speak!).[5] Has any artist ever spoken more than him? But he knew the difference between speaking and doing; it was just that he said little about his activity as an architect. Here, too, there is an obstacle in the path to understanding Loos as an architect: it is Loos the writer. In every instance, one has to look closely to determine where the writer clarifies what the architect is doing. Let us speak for a moment about the journalist Loos. From the very beginning, Loos was intent on taking on the current affairs of his day much beyond their superficial meanings. For that reason, he wrote that a single example was not important to him. He never denied the world to which he belonged and about which he wrote: "Vienna, Austria, or put more broadly Germany." When he described his journal as "a magazine for the introduction of Western culture into Austria," it showed how much he loved "this Vienna, this Austria"—and how deeply he despised them. He spent the decisive years of his early development abroad, in America. He was also in England, and he knew very well what had happened there in the applied arts since the time of William Morris. In both countries, he thought that he had found their everyday culture, especially the everyday culture of handcraft. Does he ever say anything anywhere about the skyscraper, does he ever say anything at all about industrial development in the United States? As far as I can see, he spoke only of the freer and the more dignified way in which people in the English-speaking countries confronted the necessities of life and those of art. They knew how to distinguish the one from the other. There, art does not presume to shape everyday life; there, he thought a healthy, vital, modern everyday life could be found, one that did not require a Secession. Later, because he also rejected the Werkbund, Loos made a list of those objects that were inherently modern—it is a very Austrian list:

> Our carriages, our drinking glasses, our optical instruments, our umbrellas and walking sticks, our suitcases and saddlery, our silver cigarette cases and costume jewelry, our fine jewelry and clothing are modern. They are so because no pretenders have sought to pose as guardians of these workshops.

Except for optical instruments, everything on this list is a product of handicraft, even luxury handicraft, which the Austrians were good at in those days. The problem that brought the Werkbund into being, namely the deterioration in the quality of products caused by the introduction of the machine, does not seem to have attracted Loos's attention, although he must have encountered the phenomenon, if not in Austria, then certainly in America. What is unexpected is the conservative standpoint we can detect in his writings.

Speaking of his conservative attitude, allow me to mention another development (the first was the rise of industrial production) that greatly concerned his contemporaries, but which apparently was of no interest to Loos: construction. The two central themes of the years around the turn of the century were really the problem of serial production on the one hand and, on the other, the relationship of architecture to new materials and construction methods. Loos was not truly touched by this development, either; reading his work, one comes away with the impression that architectural construction had not advanced beyond that which had served Michelangelo, or, to put it less pretentiously, the simple builders of simple houses. Loos does mention Otto Wagner, the newest star in the architectural firmament. But about the bold glass roof construction in Wagner's Postal Savings Bank, Loos has nothing to say.

Let me attempt here to clarify his attitude toward art in architecture (which is not easy): Loos rejected the influence of art on objects of everyday life, of which the house is a part. This was his dispute with the Secession. But he had no doubt that architecture was an art. His conviction here was so strong that the problem of new construction, which everyone had been discussing for decades—and with which the esteemed Otto Wagner had made some real progress—did not, as far as we know, particularly interest him. Loos committed himself to tradition, and by that he expressly meant Greco-Roman antiquity. Again and again, he states that the great architects all looked back to antiquity, that architecture, despite the periodic fluctuations of the zeitgeist, would remain the most conservative art. He names these greats: Schlüter, Fischer von Erlach, Schinkel, "the great tamer of the imagination," and Semper.

"We can therefore assert," he continues, "that the future great architect will be a classicist. One who does not rely on the works of his forbears, but, rather, directly on classical antiquity."[6]

Certainly this "classical antiquity" does have a richer formal language, legitimized by the discoveries of archeology.

It is not without amazement that one observes that this man, who constantly evoked everyday life and its forms, who spoke without hesitation about how much architects and applied artists owed to everyday life, was also the man who wanted to see that one of the lessons of architectural history was the need for a periodic disciplining of free imagination by the severity of antiquity.

So much for Loos the journalist.

But the more I let the assertions of the polemical journalist Loos pour over me, the more the points of contact between his journalism and his architecture become clear. In both realms, he saw himself as an educator. His notion of everyday life was not as Aristotelean as one might first imagine, especially in view of his constant references to the natural, the commonsense, the authentic. These are qualities that may be latent in all of us; but after experiencing a period in which taste had become so confused,[7] the natural, the commonsense, and what was supposed to be true, had to be relearned.

Most of all, however, the epoch needed a natural sense of propriety, like that of the classical antiquity: according to Loos—and others—it had been lost completely. And just as the discipline of classical antiquity had served to counter the excesses of the Baroque, it could now also serve as a corrective to the excesses of the Secession. It is not without reason that Loos called Schinkel the tamer of pure fantasy. The word "fantasy" does not necessarily connote "beauty" for him. If we look at examples of his own architecture, we also notice the high demands inherent it: first, his penchant for materials: Loos used slabs of marble—or of high-quality hardwoods—in such a way that, next to the richness of their grain, every form of applied ornament would appear meager. (It should be noted that Mies van der Rohe learned this from him.) The other claim I want to speak of is the frequent use he makes of symmetry, of axiality. Again and again, for example, we will find two cupboards and a picture in a symmetrical arrangement set on a wall, the main wall, in his rooms, and, again and again, there is a direct, conventional axiality in the plan and in the façades. When Loos talks about everyday life, he doesn't mean that one should lounge casually about one's living space. Even the hints of English ease that one encounters in his early work later disappear altogether. Whoever enters one of Loos's houses does not enter a palace; but he enters a bourgeois environment with a certain demeanor.

Not a palace: as soon as one enters the Müller House in Prague, which appears so austere on its exterior, one is on an ascending path that reveals the rooms and their relationship to one another; the Raumplan replaces the classical-hierarchical principle with one that one could paraphrase with the word "convenience," which, however, does not mean a *functional* convenience: on the contrary. Even the constant climbing of stairs in a Loos house is uncomfortable.

I'm thinking more of something like serenity: a free and generous relationship of the volumes to each other. The symmetries serve only to indicate that one should behave oneself here, regardless of the looseness of the planning. The elegant and emphatically displayed materials—marble, fine woods—also serve to underscore this. Apparently, this admixture of freedom and form was very important to Loos. Unfortunately, I have never been in the Müller House. The only experience I have had with a Loosian room sequence came with repeated visits to the salesrooms of the Kniže men's fashion store on the Graben in Vienna. Anyone finding himself in these spaces knows that one does not simply select something, pay for it, and leave. You discuss exactly what you want, you take the advice of the experienced staff, the tailor goes into action; I shouldn't be surprised if a cup of coffee would have been handed to me in Loos's time. Very old people remember this culture of buying and selling.

It belongs to the past. The same applies to the culture of expecting and receiving visitors, which must have prevailed in a house like the Villa Müller in Prague, and which elsewhere I have described with vague expressions such as "comfortable" and "calm." People today don't grasp what is going on there. But if one examines the Raumplan—and the symmetries and the beautiful materials—but especially the Raumplan, and once again the Raumplan, you can get a—faint—idea of the considered constraint that prevailed in such rooms.

On the outside, however, things looked different. One feels the hand of a man who called Schinkel the great tamer of the imagination. There is a noticeable difference between the shape of the building and the strict arrangement of the openings, on the one hand, and the relaxed, relaxing effect of the interior plan, on the other. Le Corbusier expressed this difference in relation to his own Villa Savoye:

> "On affirme, à l'extérieur, une volonté architecturale, on satisfait, à l'interieur, à tous les besoins fonctionells."[8]

That is not quite the same as what Loos was trying to do. Loos did not want to satisfy functional needs with the Raumplan, but the demands of social life. What both views have in common, however, is that they recognize the difference between outside and inside. Loos would not have accepted Häring's dictum that the shape of a house emerges of its own accord if the planning does justice to its function. Loos did say that you should plan a house from the inside out; yes, maybe this much-used formula comes from him. But look at his buildings, especially those of the late period when he had fully developed the Raumplan: they betray the interior and keep it secret. The façades are also arranged in complex ways; but their overall organization is subject to an order that does not depend on what is happening in the interior. If we speak about a *volonté architecturale*, at best, Le Corbusier could claim Loos as a predecessor; if the functionalists did that, they misunderstood him.

Loos wanted to create architecture in the purest sense. He said this often and clearly, we have quoted some of his words; but he said so many other things and insisted so strongly that the architect had to plan for people's lives that this was this ignored. It's true, he wanted to serve everyday life, including the everyday lives of ordinary people. It is also true that he wanted the freedom that a Raumplan yielded; but he connected these strivings with the observance of certain norms which, he rightly thought, could only develop in the freedom of a Raumplan; because it was not the sort of formula that a tailor might employ; it was a learned ease; not a natural one, because that doesn't exist. One thinks here of Oscar Wilde's epigram:"He was one of Nature's gentlemen: the worst kind of gentleman there is."

One might think here above all of England, a country that Loos loved and admired.
The rigorous but free unfolding of form that one sees in English design is what Adolf Loos called architecture—although he definitely did not say it that way. But if one compares what he said about the constant resurgence of antiquity with his own way of planning, i.e., the Raumplan—set in the shell of a strictly symmetrical house that is intended to be memorable—if you understand his planning as the connection between classical demands and free organization of space, then you come close to what Loos called architecture.

And with that insight, ladies and gentlemen, one probably also understands what the current Loosians—and there are quite a few of them—mean when they speak about the promise of architecture, which has yet to be fulfilled. We are currently experiencing a reaction to functionalism; we are hearing voices that are crying out for architecture. They call for sculpture and architecture—or at least a sculptural architecture—I'm thinking here of Rob Krier; others want to resurrect the elements of historical architecture.[9] Adolf Loos would not have agreed with the one approach nor with the other. But I must admit, if I am not mistaken, that in the attitude taken by the so-called rationalists in Italy, Aldo Rossi, for example, we can find something of what Loos meant. But these architects think only of classical rigor, not of the Raumplan. The combination of the Raumplan and rigor, it seems to me, is the quintessence of the Adolf Loos phenomenon.

Without a doubt, here was an architect at work from whom we can learn; at least, we can do so indirectly, because the social class Loos built for has disappeared. Whether one can agree with Loos that the great architect of the future (if there should be one) will lead architecture back to its own essence through the recourse to antiquity, I don't know. I doubt it. But this I do know: the call for freedom and for form, which Loos raised in his writings and confirmed in his work, is being heard today.

Thank you, ladies and gentlemen, for your attention.

Translated by Christopher Long

Acknowledgments

I wish to thank the many people who helped to bring this book to its finished state. I am grateful, once more, to Wolfgang Thaler, who made some of the splendid photographs for the book, including its cover. And I owe a debt of thanks to Ulli Unterweger, who aided me with the research and read and commented on the texts. Alan Posener, Julius Posener's son, kindly granted me permission to reproduce his father's essay on Loos in translation. Much more than that, though, he made many suggestions for improving the translation, and he offered compelling insight into Julius Posener's life and time, which I found enormously useful. Max Moya and Cécile Poulot read and commented on chapter 5. Florence Grant copyedited the book and made astute suggestions for its improvement. And Gia Marie Houck, my dear wife, was, as always, my sounding board and best critic.

I also want to thank all those at KANT Publishers in Prague who helped to make this book a reality. I am especially grateful to Karel Kerlický, who took this project on, and to Jiří Příhoda, who designed the book, laid out the text, and saw the work through the printing process. I also wish to express my gratitude to Eva Hrubá for her editorial work.

Lastly, I need to acknowledge a long-term debt to my esteemed colleague and friend Francesco Passanti. For years, before the pandemic, we had monthly lunches, many of them at the now-defunct restaurant Fino in Austin, where we sat, sometimes for hours, discussing the rise of modern architecture, early twentieth-century intellectual thought, contemporary historiography, and much else. In so doing, he taught me far more than he will ever realize and far more than I will ever be able to use.

Notes

Chapter 1 | A Cultural Approach Notwithstanding

1| Adolf Loos, *Trotzdem 1900–1930* (Innsbruck: Brenner-Verlag, 1931). Although the book is dated 1931, it actually appeared at the end of 1930.

2| Friedrich Nietzsche, *Ecce Homo: Wie man wird, was man ist* (Leipzig: Insel-Verlag, 1908), 89.

3| Max Nordau, *Entartung*, 2 vols. (Berlin: Carl Duncker, 1892–93).

4| Christopher Long, "The Origins and Context of Adolf Loos's 'Ornament and Crime,'" *Journal of the Society of Architectural Historians* 68, no. 2 (June 2009): 207–10.

5| Adolf Loos, "Die Überflüssigen (Deutscher Werkbund)," *März* 2, no. 15 (August 3, 1908): 185–87.

6| Ibid., 185.

7| Loos's pronouncements seem to echo Alois Riegl's notion of a *Kunstwollen*—literally, "a will to art," but more accurately expressed as a shared set of beliefs that produce a common artistic culture. Riegl, however, emphasized the unique features of each era's artistic production, something that Loos was much less interested in. Alois Riegl, *Die spatrömische Kunst-Industrie nach den Funden in Österreich-Ungarn im Zusammenhange mit der Gesamtentwicklung der Bildenden Künste bei den Mittelmeervölkern* (Vienna: Verlag der kaiserlich-königlichen Hof- und Staatsdruckerei, 1901).

8| Loos, "Die Überflüssigen," 185.

9| The reference to "modern ornament" here seemingly flies in the face of Loos's later anti-ornament pronouncements. It is, in fact, entirely consistent with his views, as I will discuss below.

10| Ibid., 186.

11| Long, "Origins and Context," 210–11.

12| Adolf Loos, "Ornament und Verbrechen," in *Trotzdem*, 82.

13| Ibid., 86.

14| Ibid., 88.

15| Ibid., 92.

16| Ibid.

17| Ibid., 89.

18| On Morký, see, e.g., Lubomír Slavíček, ed., *Slovník historiků umění, výtvarných kritiků, teoretiků a publicistů v českých zemích a jejich spolupracovníků z příbuzných oborů (asi 1800–2008)* (Prague: Academia, 2016), 1:941; and Alena Kavčáková, "Prof. akad. mal. F. V. Mokrý—umělec a výtvarný pedagog," *Acta Universitatis Palackianae Olomucensis Facultas Paedagogica, Aesthetica* VII, Výtvarná výchova 6 (1991): 81–125.

19| Adolf Loos, "Moje odpovědi k dotazníku 'Našeho směru,'" *Naš směr. Revue pro kreslení a estetickou výchovu* 11, nos. 3–4 (1924–25): 50–52.

20| Adolf Loos, "Ornament und Erziehung," in *Trotzdem*, 198–205.

21| Ibid., 200.

22| That would be 1908. But Loos, as recent scholarship has demonstrated, misremembered the date. He first wrote out a full version of "Ornament and Crime" in late 1909 or early 1910.

23| Ibid., 202–3.

Chapter 2 | The Iconic Tower

1| Katherine Solomonson, *The Chicago Tribune Competition: Skyscraper Design and Cultural Change in the 1920s* (Chicago: University of Chicago Press, 2001), 118. Solomonson cites Ludwig Münz and Gustav Künstler, *Adolf Loos: Pioneer of Modern Architecture*, trans. Harold Meek (New York: Frederick A. Praeger, 1966), 193; Manfredo Tafuri, "The Disenchanted Mountain," in *The American City from the Civil War to the New Deal*, ed. Giorgio Ciucci et al. (London: Granada, 1980), 402–3; Benedetto Gravagnuolo, *Adolf Loos: Theory and Works* (New York: Rizzoli, 1982), 174; Robert A. M. Stern, "Chicago Tribune Tower," *Architectural Design* 50 (1980): 35; Anthony Vidler, "The Big Greek Column Will Be Built: Adolf Loos and the Sign of Classicism," *Skyline* (October 1982): 16–17; and Panayotis Tournikiotis, *Adolf Loos* (New York: Princeton Architectural Press, 1994), 155. For a full account of Loos's project for the *Chicago Tribune* competition, see Burkhardt Rukschcio and Roland Schachel, *Adolf Loos: Leben und Werk*, 2nd ed. (Salzburg: Residenz Verlag, 1987): 273–77, 562–64.

2| Vidler, "Big Greek Column," 16.

3| Gravagnuolo, *Adolf Loos: Theory and Works*, 174.

4| Loos's first wife was Lina (Carolina) Obertimpfler (1882–1950). The couple married in 1902 and divorced in 1905. Loos lived with English dancer Bessie Bruce (1883–1921) off and on for nearly a decade, from 1905 to 1914—longer than he lived with any of his three wives—but they were never legally married because divorce and remarriage was forbidden in Catholic Austria before World War I. He married Elsie Altmann (1899–1984) in 1919; they divorced in 1926. Loos married his third wife, Claire Beck (1904–42), in 1929; they divorced in 1932.

5| Elsie is very far off the mark. There were five other submissions from Austria alone and more than one hundred from across Europe. Loos is listed in the section of French architects because he was then living in Paris. Another Austrian architect, Clemens Holzmeister, was erroneously listed in the German section.

6| Elsie Altmann-Loos, *Mein Leben mit Adolf Loos* (Vienna: Amalthea Signum Verlag, 2013), 148.

7| Ibid., 148–49.

8| Ibid., 149.

9| Ibid.

10| Ibid., 150.

11| Claire Loos, *Adolf Loos Privat* (Vienna: Verlag der Johannes-Presse, 1936), 111–12; translated in Claire Beck Loos, *The Private Adolf Loos: Portrait of an Eccentric Genius*, trans. Constance C. Pontasch and Nicholas Saunders (Los Angeles: DoppelHouse Press, 2020), 135–36.

12| Solomonson, *Chicago Tribune Competition*, 37.

13| Ibid., 67.

14| The promise of very large awards, totaling $100,000, drew entries from many architects abroad. Some 1,800 architects worldwide "enrolled," but only 263 eventually submitted entries. By November 1, 120 entries had arrived; judging began immediately. Over the next four weeks entries continued to trickle in; by November 30, 79 additional designs had been received. Many, including Loos's, as we have seen, came too late and were never reviewed by the jury. Loos was in good company; among the late entries were the designs of the Germans Max Taut, Bruno Taut, and Walter Gropius and Adolf Meyer.

15| Rukschcio and Schachel, *Adolf Loos: Leben und Werk*, 556.

16| Gravagnuolo, *Adolf Loos: Theory and Works, 98.*

17| Cf. Colin Rowe's *The Mathematics of the Ideal Villa and Other Essays* (Cambridge, MA: MIT Press, 1976).

18| Gravagnuolo, *Adolf Loos: Theory and Works*, 99.

19| Ludwig Münz, *Adolf Loos* (Milan: Il Balcone, 1956), 29–33; Eduard F. Sekler, "Josef Hoffmann, Adolf Loos und die Vereinigten Staaten," in *Wien und die Architektur des 20. Jahrhunderts*, ed. Elisabeth Liskar (Vienna: Hermann Böhlaus Nachf., 1986), 130–31.

20| Rukschcio and Schachel, *Adolf Loos: Leben und Werk*, 98–99.

21| Joseph Masheck, *Adolf Loos: The Art of Architecture* (London: I. B. Tauris, 2013), 151–52.

22| Ibid., 153–54.

23| "Der Internationale Wettbewerb für den Zeitungspalast der 'Chicago Tribune,'" *Zeitschrift*
24| *des Österr. Ingenieur- und Architekten–Vereines*, Heft 3/4 (January 26, 1923): 16–17.
Gravagnuolo, *Adolf Loos: Theory and Works*, 174.

25| Adolf Loos, "Ornament und Erziehung," in *Trotzdem 1900–1930* (Innsbruck: Brenner-Verlag, 1931), 203–4. Although the book is dated 1931, it actually appeared at the end of 1930.

26| Ibid., 204.

27| Rukschcio and Schachel, *Adolf Loos: Leben und Werk*, 242, 247, 249, 581.

Chapter 3 | Adolf Loos and the Lessons of the Vernacular

1| Adolf Loos, "Ueber Architektur," *Der Sturm* 1 (1910): 334.

2| Adolf Loos, "L'Architecture et le style modern," *Les Cahiers d'aujourd'hui* 2 (December 1912): 82–92.

3| Adolf Loos, "Architektur," in *Trotzdem 1900–1930* (Innsbruck: Brenner-Verlag, 1931), 95–113. Although the book is dated 1931, it actually appeared at the end of 1930.

4| Ibid., 111–12. All translations are my own.

5| Ibid., 111.

6| Ibid., 95.

7| Ibid

8| Ibid., 98.

9| Ibid., 96.

10| Ibid., 99.

11| Adolf Loos, "Regeln für den, der in den Bergen baut," *Jahrbuch der Schwarzwald'schen Schulanstalten* (1913): 25. The essay was reprinted in *Der Brenner* 4, no. 1 (1913): 40.

12| Ibid

13| Ibid

14| Loos, "Architektur," 105–6.

15| Ibid., 106.

16| Burkhardt Rukschcio and Roland Schachel, *Adolf Loos: Leben und Werk*, 2nd ed. (Salzburg: Residenz Verlag, 1987), 497.

17| Ibid., 565.

18| Khuner was the son of Gottfried Friedrich Khuner (1854–1912), who, together with his father, Emanuel Mendel Khuner (1829–85), founded a company that manufactured cooking fats. In Atzgersdorf, then just outside Vienna, they established a factory in 1895 and began producing an early form of margarine they named "Kunerol," on which the family fortune was based. On the Khuner House, see Rukschcio and Schachel, *Adolf Loos: Leben und Werk*, 617–22. The project is documented in ALA 68, 69, 291, 305–9, 443, 881–85. Some records relating to the house are also in the Bauamt Payerbach, Niederösterreich. For a more recent and thoroughgoing study of the house, see Markus Kristan, *Adolf Loos—Landhaus Khuner am Kreuzberg* (Vienna: Höhere Graphische Bundes-Lehr– u. Versuchsanstalt, 2004). Loos also designed and erected a gardener's cottage on the property in a related style. See ALA 623 and ALA 2268.

19| On the Raumplan features of the house, see Christopher Long, *The New Space: Movement and Experience in Viennese Modern Architecture* (New Haven, CT: Yale University Press, 2016), 161–73.

20| Michael Falser, "Das Landhaus Khuner von Adolf Loos am Semmering/Niederösterreich (1929/30)—Eine bau- und stilgeschichtliche Einordnung," *kunsttexte.de* (2005), 3, 8–9.

21| Heinrich Kulka, *Adolf Loos: Das Werk des Architekten* (Vienna: Anton Schroll, 1931), 13–15.

22| Hermann Muthesius, *Das englische Haus: Entwicklung, Bedingungen-Anlage, Aufbau, Einrichtung und Innenraum*, 3 vols. (Berlin: Ernst Wasmuth, 1908–11). Dušan Jurkovič used a very similar concept in his own house in Brno, likely also taken in part from Muthesius's work.

Chapter 4 | Julius Posener on Adolf Loos

1| Julius Posener, "Der Raumplan: Vorläufer und Zeitgenossen von Adolf Loos," in *Adolf Loos 1870–1933: Raumplan–Wohnungsbau*, ed. Dietrich Worbs, exh. cat. (Berlin: Akademie der Künste, 1983), 52–63.

2| Alan Posener, email to the author, June 10, 2022.

3| Ibid. Erich Blunck (1872–1950) was conservative architect and historic preservationist who taught at the Technische Hochschule in Berlin-Charlottenburg from 1907 to 1945, and again from 1947 to the time of his death. Heinrich Tessenow (1876–1950) was one of the architects of the prewar *Gartenstadt* (Garden City) in Dresden-Hellerau; later, he became one of the leading exponents of the *Heimatstil* or nativist style that strongly influenced the direction of German architecture during the Third Reich.

4| Ibid.

5| Ibid.

6| Julius Posener, *Mein Leben mit der Architektur* (Berlin: Aedes Galerie und Architekturforum, 1989), 28.

7| See, e.g., Paul Goldberger, "Julius Posener, an Architect and Critic of Modern Movement," *New York Times*, January 31, 1996, section B, 6.

8| Alan Posener, email to the author, June 10, 2022.

9| I do not know when Johnson first made the statement, but one of the most public occasions was during his 1957 address "100 Years, Frank Lloyd Wright, and Us," delivered to the Washington State Chapter of the American Institute of Architects in Seattle. The talk was later published in *Pacific Architect and Builder* 1 (March 1957): 35–36.

10| Julius Posener, *Adolf Loos 1870–1933: Ein Vortrag* (Berlin: Akademie der Künste, 1984), 5–6.

11| Ibid., 12.

12| Josef Hoffmann, "The Workprogram of the Wiener Werkstätte 1903 / Programm der Wiener Werksätte 1903," in *Josef Hoffmann: Architect and Designer 1870–1956* (Vienna: Galerie Metropol, 1981), 7–22. Hoffmann begins the piece in a way that leaves no doubt about his and Koloman Moser's intentions in founding the Wiener Werkstätte: "The boundless evil, caused by shoddy mass-produced goods and by the uncritical imitation of earlier styles, is like a tidal wave sweeping across the world."

13| See, e.g., Hans Puchhammer, "Adolf Loos als Konstrukteur," in *Adolf Loos*, ed. Burkhardt Rukschcio, exh. cat. (Vienna: Graphische Sammlung Albertina, 1989), 173–90.

14| Posener, *Adolf Loos 1870–1933: Ein Vortrag*, 13.

15| Ibid., 15.

16| Ibid., 16.

Chapter 5 | Adolf Loos and His Contemporaries

1| Andreas Nierhaus and Alfred Pfoser, *Meine angebetete Louise! Otto Wagner: Das Tagebuch des Architekten 1915–1918* (Salzburg: Residenz Verlag, 2019).

2| Ibid., 133.

3| Felix Augenfeld, "Erinnerungen an Adolf Loos," *Bauwelt* 72 (November 6, 1981): 1907.

4| Ludwig Hevesi, "Kunst auf der Straße," in *Acht Jahre Sezession (März 1897–Juni 1905): Kritik–Polemik–Chronik* (Vienna: Verlagsbuchhandlung Carl Konegen, 1906), 174–75.

5| Ludwig Hevesi, "Biedermeier und Komp.," in *Altkunst–Neukunst: Wien 1894–1908* (Vienna: Verlagsbuchhandlung Carl Konegen, 1909), 190.

6| Ludwig Hevesi, "Adolf Loos," in *Altkunst–Neukunst*, 285.

7| Ludwig Hevesi, "Der Neubau des Kriegsministeriums," in *Altkunst–Neukunst*, 299.

8| Hugo Wittmann, "Das Haus gegenüber der Burg," *Neue Freie Presse*, December 4, 1910, 1–2. On the larger controversy surrounding the building and its design, see Christopher Long, *The Looshaus* (New Haven, CT: Yale University Press, 2011), esp. chapter 8.

9| Long, *The Looshaus*, 107.

10| Karl Rykl, "Stenographischer Bericht über die öffentliche Sitzung des Gemeinderates vom 22. [*sic*] Oktober 1910," *Amtsblatt der k.k. Reichshaupt- und Residenzstadt Wien* 19, no. 85 (October 25, 1910): 2558.

11| Emil Szittya, *Das Kuriositäten-Kabinett* (Konstanz: See-Verlag, 1923), 289.

12| Long, *The Looshaus*, esp. chapter 10.

13| Karl Marilaun, *Adolf Loos* (Vienna: Wiener Literarische Anstalt, 1922), 9.

14| Adolf Loos, *Wohnungswanderungen* (Vienna, 1907).

15| Christopher Long, "The Origins and Context of Adolf Loos's 'Ornament and Crime,'" *Journal of the Society of Architectural Historians* 68, no. 2 (June 2009): 202–5, 211–12, 214–15.

16| Burkhardt Rukschcio and Roland Schachel, *Adolf Loos: Leben und Werk*, 2nd ed. (Salzburg: Residenz Verlag, 1987), 147–48, 176–80.

17| Adolf Loos, "Lob der Gegenwart," *März: Halbmonatschrift der deutsche Kultur* 2, no. 3 (1908): 310–12; "Kultur," *März: Halbmonatschrift der deutsche Kultur* 2, no. 4 (1908): 134–36; "Die Überfüssigen," *März: Halbmonatschrift der deutsche Kultur* 2, no. 15 (1908): 185–87.

18| Szittya, *Das Kuriositäten-Kabinett*, 289.

19| Adolf Loos, "Ornement et crime," trans. Marcel Ray, *Les Cahiers d'aujour-d'hui* 5 (June 1913): 247–56.

20| On the publication history of "Ornament and Crime," see Long, "Origins and Context," esp. 215–18.

21| Rukschcio and Schachel, *Adolf Loos: Leben und Werk*, 247–49.

22| The book of essays appeared a year later, in 1921: Adolf Loos, *Ins Leere gesprochen 1897–1900* (Paris: Éditions George Crès, 1921).

23| Adolf Loos, "Ornement et crime," *L'Esprit nouveau* 2 (November 1920): 159–68.

24| Rukschcio and Schachel, *Adolf Loos: Leben und Werk*, 295.

25| Cécile Poulot, "Adolf Loos a Vienne, Paris et Prague: Habiter l'Europe de l'entre-deux-guerres" (PhD diss., Université Sorbonne Nouvelle, Paris, 2020).

26| See, e.g., Martina Hrabová, *Galaxie Le Corbusier, Svět přátel z pařížského ateliéru na fotografiích ze sbírky Františka Sammera* (Prague: Artefactum, 2021).

27| Rukschcio and Schachel, *Adolf Loos: Leben und Werk*, 359–65.

28| The title page of the book bears the date 1931, but the work appeared at the very end of 1930.

29| Max Moya, "Who Has Seen Adolf Loos? Images of Adolf Loos's Architecture in the Media, 1899–1927" (PhD diss., Akademie der bildenden Künste Wien, 2021).

30| Ibid., 188.

31| Ibid., 472–78.

32| Richard Pommer and Christian F. Otto, *Weissenhof 1927 and the Modern Movement in Architecture* (Chicago: University of Chicago Press, 1991), esp. chapters 6 and 13.

33| See, e.g., his comments in "Josef Veillich," *Frankfurter Zeitung*, March 21, 1929, reprinted in Adolf Loos, *Trotzdem 1900–1930* (Innsbruck: Brenner-Verlag, 1931), 248–49.

34| Rukschcio and Schachel, *Adolf Loos: Leben und Werk*, 51–52; 104–6.

35| Christopher Long, *Adolf Loos on Trial* (Prague: Kant, 2017), esp. chapter 4; Czech language ed. *Případ Adolf Loos* (Brno: Barrister & Principal, 2017).

36| Ernst A. Plischke, interview by author, November 17, 1986.

1| Armand Weiser, "Berichtigung: Zum Loosbuch," *Die Bau- und Werkkunst* (January 1932): 148.

2| Heinrich Kulka, *Adolf Loos: Das Werk des Architekten* (Vienna: Verlag von Anton Schroll, 1931). Weiser's original review had appeared in the June 1931 issue of the journal. Armand Weiser, "Buchbesprechung," *Die Bau- und Werkkunst* (June 1931): supplement.

3| Kulka, Münz, and Glück write: "Es ist unwahr, daß vom 'freien Denken im Raum' als Gegensatz zu einem 'wohldurchstudierten Grundriß' geschprochen wird, wahr ist, daß der genau definierte Raumplan zum Grundriß in Bezeihung gesetzt ist." Weiser response to this is—predictably—dismissive: "Das Kapitel 'Der Raumplan ist und bleibt Literatur. Wenn Loos Räume in verschiedenen Niveaus angeordent hat, hier mit Nutzen, dort mit Schaden, kam deshalb denoch 'kein neuer, höherer Raumgedanke zur Welt.'" Weiser, "Berichtigung: Zum Loosbuch," 148.

4| One other short book, an "appreciation" of Loos by Karl Marilaun, *Adolf Loos* (Vienna: Wiener Literarische Anstalt, 1922), appeared during Loos's life, but it dealt almost exclusively with his personality and views rather than his architecture.

5| Adolf Loos, "Josef Veillich," *Frankfurter Zeitung*, March 21, 1929, reprinted in *Trotzdem 1900–1930* (Innsbruck: Brenner-Verlag, 1931), 248–49. Although the book is dated 1931, it actually appeared at the end of 1930.

6| Henry [Heinrich] Kulka, "Adolf Loos, 1870–1933," *Architects' Year Book* (London) 9 (1960): 7–29.

7| See, for example, Tanja Poppelreuter, "Raumplan after Loos: The European Work of Heinrich Kulka, 1930–1939," *Fabrications: The Journal of the Society of Architectural Historians, Australia and New Zealand* 25, no. 1 (January 2015): 84–103; I. V. Porsolt, "Henry Kulka, Architect 1900–1971," *Landfall: A New Zealand Quarterly* 99 (September 1971): 289–94; and Charles Richard Goldie, "Henry Kulka" (MA thesis, University of Auckland, 1986).

8| Kulka, "Adolf Loos, 1870–1933," 15.

9| Ibid.

10| Ibid.

11| Ibid.

12| Ludwig Münz and Gustav Künstler, *Der Architekt Adolf Loos: Darstellung seines Schaffens nach Werkgruppen / Chronologisches Werkverzeichnis* (Vienna: Verlag Anton Schroll, 1964).

13| Ibid., 15.

14| Ludwig Münz and Gustav Künstler, *Adolf Loos: Pioneer of Modern Architecture*, trans. Harold Meek (New York: Frederick A. Praeger, 1966), 139.

15| Ibid., 140.

16| Kulka, *Adolf Loos: Das Werk des Architekten*, 13.

17| Christopher Long, *The New Space: Movement and Experience in Viennese Modern Architecture* (New Haven, CT: Yale University Press, 2016).

18| Greta Knutson, "Das Haus Tristan Tzara," *Bauwelt* 42 (June 11, 1981), 1896–97.

1| Bořivoj Kriegerbeck to Zdeněk Kudělka, November 4, 1968, SDC-MV-MMP-ZK, Villa Müller Study and Documentation Center, City of Prague, quoted in Jindřich Chatrný, Dagmar Černoušková, Jana Kořínková, and Karel Zoch, eds., *On, Adolf Loos—Bořivoj Kriegerbeck—On Adolf Loos* (Brno: Muzeum města Brna, Fakulta výtvarných umění Vysokého učení technického v Brně, Archiv města Brna, 2001), 36. Here Kriegerbeck is referring to Otto Beck (1869–1936). Throughout the text, he mistakenly calls him Josef.

2| Chatrný et al., *On, Adolf Loos*, 33–34.

3| Ibid., 201–2.

4| Ibid., 204–5.

5| Claire later published a detailed and sometimes harrowing account of her time with Loos. Claire Loos, *Adolf Loos Privat* (Vienna: Verlag der Johannes-Presse, 1936); English ed. Claire Beck Loos, *The Private Adolf Loos: Portrait of an Eccentric Genius*, trans. Constance C. Pontasch and Nicholas Saunders (Los Angeles: DoppelHouse Press, 2020).

6| Chatrný et al., *On, Adolf Loos*, 162.

7| Ibid., 148.

8| Ibid., 150.

9| Ibid., 166.

10| On Loos's arrest and trial, see Christopher Long, *Adolf Loos on Trial* (Prague: Kant, 2017); Czech language ed. *Případ Adolf Loos* (Brno: Barrister & Principal, 2017).

11| Chatrný et al., *On, Adolf Loos*, 136.

12| Ibid., 154.

13| Christopher Long, "Adolf Loos, Winternitzova vila a otázka autorství /Adolf Loos, Villa Winternitz, and the Question of Authorship," in *Vila Jenny a Josefa Winternitzových / The Villa of Jenny and Josef Winternitz: Adolf Loos, Karel Lhota 1931–1932*, ed. Lada Hubatová-Vacková and Valentyna Nikolenko (Prague: UMPRUM / Vysoká škola uměleckoprůmyslová v Praze, 2020), 54–75.

14| Jindřich Chatrný, Dagmar Černoušková, and Jana Kořínková, eds., *Evropan Adolf Loos, Nejen brněnske stopy / Adolf Loos, European: His Legacy in Brno and Beyond*, exh. cat. (Brno: Muzeum města Brna and Fakulta výtvarných umění Vysokého učení technického v Brně, 2020).

15| Pavel Borský and Dagmar Černoušková, "Vzpomínka na profesora Zdeňka Kudělku," *ZPP, časopis státní památkové péče* (2001): 52–53; Lubomír Slavíček, "Soupis prací Zdeňka Kudělky II," *Sborník prací Filozofické fakulty brněnské univerzity* 50, čís. F45 (2001): 113–14.

16| For the full essay, see Zdeněk Kudělka, "Pojetí obývaného prostoru u Adolfu Loose," *Umění* 31, no. 1 (1983): 59–72.

17| Chatrný, Černoušková, and Kořínková, *Evropan Adolf Loos*, 425.

18| Ibid.

19| Ibid.

20| The passage appears in a short remembrance Loos wrote of his favorite cabinetmaker, Josef Veillich, who had recently died: "Before Immanuel Kant, people could not think spatially, and architects were forced to make the toilet as high as the formal hall. Only by means of dividing the space in half could they succeed in making lower rooms. And just as we will one day play three-dimensional chess, so other architects will be able in the future to dissolve the ground plan into space." Adolf Loos, "Josef Veillich," *Frankfurter Zeitung*, March 21, 1929, reprinted in *Trotzdem 1900–1930* (Innsbruck: Brenner-Verlag, 1931), 248–49.

21| Chatrný, Černoušková, and Kořínková, *Evropan Adolf Loos*, 425–26.

22| Ibid., 136–38.

Chapter |8 Adolf Loos, We Hardly Knew Ye: An Obituary

1| Jonathan Lighter, *The Best Anti-War Song Ever Written, Occasional Papers in Folklore 1* (Windsor, NJ: CAMSCO Music, Loomis House Press, 2012).

2| F.R.Y. [Maxwell Fry], "Adolf Loos," *Architect & Building News* 136 (October 13, 1933): 32.

3| Ibid.

4| It is possible that this is a corruption of the Czech phrase "v Brně," in Brno.

5| Heinrich Kulka, *Adolf Loos: Das Werk des Architekten* (Vienna: Verlag von Anton Schroll, 1931).

Appendix | Adolf Loos 1870–1933: A Lecture, by Julius Posener

1| The exhibition was *Adolf Loos 1870–1933: Raumplan–Wohnungsbau*, organized by Dietrich Worbs and held at the Berlin Akademie der Künste, from December 4, 1983, to January 15, 1984.

2| Posener is referring here to the period of the 1870s and 1880s, the time of German unification and afterward, when rapid industrialization and the new aesthetic of historicism were developing hand in hand.

3| Adolf Loos, "Josef Veillich," *Frankfurter Zeitung*, March 21, 1929, reprinted in *Trotzdem 1900–1930* (Innsbruck: Brenner-Verlag, 1931), 248–49.

4| Adolf Loos, "Vom armen reichen Mann," *Neues Wiener Tagblatt*, April 26, 1900, 1–2, reprinted in *Adolf Loos, Ins Leere gesprochen 1897–1900* (Paris: Éditions Georges Crès, 1921), 159–63.

5| The quotation is from Goethe, who repeated it frequently in his writings and conversations.

6| The quotation is from Loos's essay "Die alte und die neue Richtung in der Baukunst," *Der Architekt* 4, no. 4 (1898): 31–32.

7| Posener is alluding to the period of late historicism when the problem of artifice versus what was purportedly "real" and "true" had come to the fore.

8| "We affirm, on the outside, an architectural will, we satisfy, on the inside, all the functional needs."

9| Posener is pointing explicitly at those postmodernists, like Robert Venturi and Charles Moore, who were calling for a return to historical form languages, or least an ongoing visual discourse with them.

Christopher Long | Adolf Loos: Meaning, Context, Reception
Essays

This book was published with assistance from the Martin S. Kermacy Endowment, School of Architecture, University of Texas at Austin.

Cover photograph: Detail of the interior marble cladding of Adolf Loos' Goldman & Salatsch Building, Vienna, 1909–11. Photograph by Wolfgang Thaler

Graphic design and the picture editing:
| Jiří Příhoda
Publisher:
| Karel Kerlický – KANT 2022, Prague
www.kant-books.com

KANT

Print:
| Tiskárna Protisk, s.r.o., Czech Republic

ISBN: 978-7437-395-4